**MOUNTAINEERS
OUTDOOR EXPERT**

series

SNOWSHOEING
Fifth Edition

Gene Prater

Edited by Dave Felkley

THE MOUNTAINEERS BOOKS

Published by
The Mountaineers Books
1001 SW Klickitat Way, Suite 201
Seattle, WA 98134

First edition 1974. Second edition 1980. Third edition 1988. Fourth edition: first printing 1997, second printing 1998. Fifth edition 2002.

Published simultaneously in Great Britain by Cordee, 3a DeMontfort Street, Leicester, England LE1 7HD

Manufactured in the United States of America

Copyediting: Watershed Books
Illustration: Hans Neuhart
Cover and book design: The Mountaineers Books
Typography and book layout: Watershed Books
All photographs by Gene Prater unless otherwise noted

Cover photograph: *Snowshoes walking on mountain* © EyeWire
Back cover photograph: © 2002 Keoki Flagg for Atlas Show-Shoe Co.

Cataloging-in-publication data on file at the Library of Congress

Contents

Preface to the Fifth Edition

Since the appearance of the third edition of Gene Prater's book in 1988, snowshoeing has experienced a rediscovery and enjoyed increased popularity. *Snowshoeing* has long been considered the authority on the sport, but with so many changes in the industry, the book was becoming out of date. Gene died suddenly in 1993, before he could undertake the necessary revisions, so The Mountaineers Books approached me with the task of revising his text. I was honored to be asked to update this classic.

Gene's book was my introduction to snowshoeing, and little did I know how much more I was about to learn by undertaking this project. From my years of snowshoeing experience, along with the research for this editing project, I have found that although new ideas and equipment have been important, the basic principles of snowshoeing—which come naturally from wanting to walk in snow—are the same after 6,000 years. And the snowflakes of winter have not changed at all.

I first met Gene's daughter, Connie Prater, and his son, Eric Prater, to discuss the book and their father, which helped me tremendously to retain the flavor of the book and character of the man I had never met. Thanks to you both and also to Gene's brother, Bill Prater, and former wife, Yvonne Prater, who have been most helpful with insights into Gene's earlier years. Even though Gene and I never met, I now stay in contact with his family and have realized that if we haven't been on the trail together in a past life, we will be in the next one.

The help on this fifth edition came in two categories: a new chapter on history and many additional new photographs. The basis of the snowshoe history being expanded into its own chapter comes from an out-of-print book, *The Snowshoe Book,* (third edition, 1983) by William E. Osgood and Leslie Hurley, originally published by the former Stephen Greene Press. It has been my other snowshoe reference book since my own snowshoe beginnings. I tracked Bill, now retired and the surviving co-author, to a small community in northwestern Vermont. Thanks to Bill's enthusiastic help and permission, many of the words on the older history are his, since he did it so well.

Those other contributors supplying the more "modern" history that is blended into the new chapter include Bill Prater, Yvonne Prater, Connie Prater, Carl Heilman, Ed Kiniry, Kathy Murphy, Lynn Cariffe, Kris Koprowski, Tom Sobel, Karen Righthand, Dave Powers "The Mountain Man," and my on-snow companions, Malcolm Stephens and Bill Opdyke. Special thanks go to my technical adviser and consultant, Skip Greene, retired/active, of Rocky Mountain Rescue and a specialist in mountain operations.

The responsibility for the second category, the photographs, was new to me. I could not have done it without the many photos supplied by Tubbs Snowshoe Company, Redfeather Snowshoes, Atlas Snow Shoe Company, the artistic photos from Carl Heilman, the illustrative action photos taken by Malcolm Stephens, and the historic photo from the Nancy Kavanagh Collection. I also included material from my own BIGfoot Snowshoe Tour slide show. Thank you all for the enticing scenes, alluring locations, and descriptive images.

Deb Easter is the new-editions coordinator who enticed me out of retirement and talked me into editing the fifth edition. My managing editor, Kathleen Cubley, kept me on track—within reason—even though I am among the few writers out there who don't like to use computers. The Business Connection, in my small mountain town of Nederland, Colorado, allowed technology to catch up with my preferred forty-five-year-old mechanical Royal typewriter. Dave White and Bill Eikenberry alleviated my frustrations with their modern wonders of electronics and computers. Thanks to you all for your understanding and knowledge.

Sales figures for snowshoes are still increasing at such a rate that if I were to record the current numbers they would be obsolete by the time this book is in print. The manufacturers of what we now call modern Western snowshoes have increased from just a few to at least two dozen since the third edition. The traditional laced wood-frame showshoes are

---

BIGfoot Says ▶▶

This sidebar is a new feature for the fifth edition. After many years of being on the snow, teaching and learning through my own BIGfoot Snowshoe Tours, there is much information to share, emphasize, or reinforce. Throughout the book you will find observations, discoveries, tips, and factoids that will make your snowshoeing experience more enjoyable, a little easier, and even safer. Take mental notes—the quiz will be on the snow.

still being made, but their sales percentage is declining, while new companies are competing for better designs, lower prices, and more customer sales. Increased competition will be to the consumer's advantage, and will probably weed out those companies that make inferior products or products that don't give good value relative to cost. However, the old-style wood-frame snowshoes will still be sold and used, since many snowshoers continue to prefer this traditional form.

The reader should be aware that even after the printing of this fifth edition, more changes will be coming in design. In order to compensate for the unknown, remember that the snowshoe design is basic and that snowflakes still fall, so this text is written to be flexible. With knowledge from this book, a newcomer to snowshoeing should be able to ask the right questions and apply the answers to what is new—then, whether novice or master, head for the new-fallen snow to have some fun.

—Dave Felkley

Gene Prater's Preface to His Third Edition

"Those are funny-looking things on your feet. What do you use them for?"

"These are snowshoes. They have a light frame with webbing or decking laced to it. I strap them to my boots and they are large enough so I can walk on the snow without sinking very deep. It's kind of dismal and depressing to be stuck indoors all winter. I really enjoy a snow hike to remind me that my world doesn't shrink down to surfaced roads and cities just because there's some snow on the ground."

Snowshoers are always explaining what snowshoes are. Laced wood-frame snowshoes have been around for centuries, but some explanation is helpful when you see what I call Western-type snowshoes for the first time. Metal frames and solid decking are a change from the traditional construction and materials.

Experienced snowshoers are fountains of wisdom about how to get around in the rugged backcountry as well. Countless times the same jewels of advice are repeated: "Say, if you kick your snowshoes deeper so the traction bites in, you won't slip." Or, "Why don't you take it easier? Often a little finesse is better than brute strength and muscle on snow." It seemed reasonable to me to collect all these jewels and put them in one place.

Recreational snowshoeing today is different from the original uses of snowshoes by the native North American, and from the uses by the trapper you envision snowshoeing along a trapline in the north woods. Generally speaking, traditional snowshoe designs work best in gentle terrain. New Englanders, however, use small snowshoes with flat toes for their steepest climbing. But for steep country everywhere, the more recent Western design is replacing the old wood models.

Don't misinterpret what I say. As I travel in the Snow Belt, I do see Western snowshoes being used more and more in territory where once only pre-1970s, wood-frame laced snowshoes were seen. However, there are vast, gentler areas where the traditional models are still in the majority.

As I travel to different areas of the North American Snow Belt and snowshoe with the local experts, I observe new or different techniques. The third edition includes many additions to the original *Snowshoeing.* It's easier to learn a new skill or activity if someone helps you take the first steps. The simplest binding looks like a tangle at first glance. The purpose of this little book is to encourage you to not only become a beginner but to continue on to a high level of expertise. There are numerous books telling about the easy parts of snow hiking or camping. I hope the information in this volume will help when winter travel is difficult.

Commercial products are treated equally in this book, in that trade names are avoided. Generic terms are used whenever possible to help a beginner choose equipment that is of good quality and works well in winter, without promoting sales of a particular make. To do so would be contrary to the policy of The Mountaineers and may create doubts about the objectivity of the book. Furthermore, it is still possible that an adept and perceptive snowshoer can make a home workshop snowshoe as good as, if not better than, anything on the market now.

When I took my first steps on snowshoes, solitude began about a quarter mile from any road. Things have changed in the over forty years since that experience. The outdoors— summer or winter—has been "sold" to the outdoor-oriented public as beneficial to health if not the solution to mankind's age-old problems of self-confidence and love of one's neigh- bors. A lot more people are out playing in the snow, and popular places may be crowded on weekends now.

Reach out to help beginners feel at home in the winter landscape. Most of us live and work in impersonal cities or suburbs where people don't want to get to know each other very well. It can add enjoyment to a winter outing to reverse this ethic and enjoy the warmth of human companionship.

As the years fly by I notice some gaps in the circle of outdoor-type friends I have enjoyed over the past years. I have benefitted from many friendships and certain people made otherwise mediocre outings noteworthy and even outstanding. Memories of these friends now gone are still vivid because we walked or worked together side by side. Their special personalities are tied to a certain place and time, adding life and vitality to experi- ences that otherwise would fade as the years pass. Even when I hike by myself, I am not alone: through the medium of memory, I see in the sunset the faces of special friends and hear their voices in the wind.

I wish to thank the following people for providing information through the third edition of this book: Don Anderson, Frank Ashley, Candice and George Bosworth, Joel Braatz, Joan

Brady, Fred Camphausen, Jim and Ann Cody, Roy Harniss, Trudy Healy, Buck Hulse, Tim Kneeland, Jerry Koch, Serge Lebell, Kathie Le Clair, Vince Lee, Rob Newcomb, Bill Prater, Glenn Prozak, Bill and Virginia Swim, Dick Tucker, Jim Tucker, Laura and Gary Waterman, Dyke Williams, and Norman Wilson.

And special thanks to my editor, Christine Deavel, who put a polish and shine on my disorganized and rough manuscript.

I encourage you to get out in winter and learn to enjoy the woods and mountains for their qualities of beauty, solitude, and grandeur, and to take time to make friends with the people who share the adventure with you. Don't be deluded into thinking it's the fashionable clothing you wear or the speed of your over-snow travel device that provides the pleasure. It isn't. The outstanding part of your outing, the part that is memorable and enduring, is the backcountry and the good companions who accompany you.

My best for a great winter experience.

—Gene Prater

CHAPTER 1

The History of Snowshoeing

This new chapter will give you a historical connection of the old to the new. It should tie the early webs of rawhide and wood to the space-age synthetics and aluminum, and into the new century, and millennium, of the even more modern Western snowshoe.

Although no one knows for sure when the first snowshoe was devised, it was probably about 6,000 years ago. The wood-frame, rawhide-laced models we now regard as "old" or "original" designs are modern compared with even earlier examples. Archaeological evidence indicates that the forerunner of the laced snowshoe was a solid slab of wood. This is a crude device compared with the museum-piece snowshoe, finely crafted of straight-grain wood and lacing as delicate as a crocheted tablecloth.

◀◀ ▲ *Ridgetop and rock tower, Lassen Volcanic National Park, California*

The earliest examples of solid-slab snowshoes are from central Asia. Perhaps some of these snowshoes were carried across the Aleutian land bridge by migrants to North America. Ancestors of the Eskimos and Indians of present-day Alaska and Canada modified the solid slab to the laced frame snowshoes still used today.

BIGfoot Says ▶▶
The following account of snowshoeing history is directly from *The Snowshoe Book* by William E. Osgood and Leslie Hurley, third edition, 1983, from "Early Beginnings" through his "Snowshoe Hikes."

EARLY BEGINNINGS

The use of snowshoes dates back over an incredibly long span of human history. Archaeologists have been unable to date the origin of either skis or snowshoes, but the best evidence suggests that the first device to serve as a foot extender for easier travel over the snow originated in central Asia about 4000 B.C. Thus the snowshoe/ski is one of the oldest inventions of man, ranking in importance with the wheel, a summer invention.

Without the snowshoe/ski, aboriginal peoples would not have been able to expand over, and occupy, the northern hemisphere. Once this important contribution to technology had been made, certain human groups began their northward migrations, which eventually enabled them to move from a central point somewhere in Asia into what are now known as Scandinavia, Siberia, and the Americas.

Asia and the Americas were once joined by land at the place where the Bering Strait now separates the United States from the [former] Soviet Union. It was then that the various predecessors of the American Indian and the Eskimo moved into the Americas. This eastward migration bridge apparently became the demarcation point between the use of snowshoes and skis. The westward-moving peoples evidently favored the ski, for, in the course of human history, skis became the favored means of transportation in northern Asia and Europe. Interchange between Asia and the Americas in the region of the Bering Strait declined, and these two human populations developed independently, each with its own culture. Interestingly enough, the snowshoe became a major part of the North American cultural heritage.

INDIANS AS INNOVATORS

Indians, as distinguished from Eskimos, were the great innovators in snowshoe design. Indians tended to move into the forested temperate zone, where snowshoes were an absolute necessity for getting around in wintertime. Eskimos, living in the polar regions, did not find snowshoes essential for they traveled mostly over sea ice or on the wind-packed snow of the tundra. Accordingly, snowshoes are not too often seen among Eskimo groups.

The Athabascan Indians of the Northwest and the Algonquin Indians of the Northeast, as well as the powerful League of the Iroquois, brought the snowshoe to the greatest peak of perfection. Starting with a basic bearpaw design, they introduced hundreds of variant patterns suited to all possible conditions. Before the horse was reintroduced to America by the Spaniards, even the Plains Indians used showshoes to hunt buffalo, and it could be truly said that one common cultural characteristic of all the Indian tribes in any region where snow covered the ground in wintertime was the snowshoe.

Insofar as we know from the Norse sagas, the first white men to set foot in North America, led by Leif Eriksson around A.D. 1000, made no mention of snowshoes being used by the Indian groups they came upon. But there is no question that snowshoe travel was well established at that time by Indians in Labrador and on Newfoundland. This is a curious omission in the otherwise detailed sagas.

Probably the first white people to make extensive adaptation of the snowshoe were the French who began to move in and colonize the St. Lawrence River area in the 1600s. The French tended to intermingle freely with the Indians, and they quickly learned how to make best use of the snowshoe in wintertime and canoe in summer. The great heroes of the French colonial period, d'Iberville, Le Moyen, Hertel de Rouville, de Nantel, and many others, were experienced snowshoers. During the prolonged French and Indian War, the struggle between French and English for dominion in North America was almost swayed to the side of the French by their superior tactics and by the way they, with their Indian allies, used snowshoes as a tactical aid for making lightning raids on English settlements.

English and Dutch pioneers moving into the hinterlands also made use of Indian lore and skills to maintain their settlements in the face of French opposition. In 1690 a group of French and Indians attacked a community near what is now Schenectady, New York, taking both prisoners and house-hold goods. The settlers gathered their forces and pursued the marauders over fifty miles on snowshoes, and recovered the prisoners and stolen goods after heavy fighting. Another person who learned well from the Indians was Robert Rogers, who put his knowledge to good use as a scout for the English armies fighting on the borderlands. The famous 1758 Battle on Snowshoes near Lake George in the Adirondacks reinforced the need for military supply officers to include snow-shoes as part of the logistical support for winter warfare. In the state papers of Vermont, for example, there are several references to payments made to furnish the militia with snowshoes.

During the great westward expansion period, snowshoes were equally as important as the ax and flintlock rifle in the zones where snow lay deep throughout the winter season. Trappers, hunters, explorers, and surveyors in these areas found snowshoes to be indispensable.

Both the Indians and the white men in these times usually made their own snowshoes according to the patterns that had been defined by the Indians long before the white men came to North America. The making of snowshoes was a home industry for the most part, although certain people who had a particular knack for the craft probably made some snowshoes for sale or barter.

Indian groups maintained the lead in snowshoe manufacture until very recent times, and even now some of the best and least expensive snowshoes are made in Indian communities. A good example of this industry is the little village of Indian Lorette, a short distance north of Quebec City, where descendants of the Huron tribe still make an excellent product for sale in Canada and the United States.

THE SPREAD OF THE SKI

Historically then, the snowshoe was dominant in North America until sometime in the 1800s when immigrating Norwegians, Swedes, and Finns introduced the ski. The process of the cultural diffusion of the ski was slow at first. Indians and the white men who preceded the Scandinavians continued to prefer the snowshoe until the 1930s, when skiing began to make its phenomenal rise as a major form of recreation. Even then, the form of skiing that took precedence was the downhill sport, with some means of mechanical transport to get the skier to the top of the slope. Snowshoeing continued to be the principal means of utilitarian travel for trappers, hunters, and woodsmen as well as for significant numbers of people who just liked to wander around in the winter forests for pure pleasure. It was not until the late 1960s that the use of skis for touring began to be popular in the United States and Canada.

THE SNOWSHOE CLUBS

Despite the rising popularity of other forms of winter recreation, snowshoes have certainly not been displaced. This is especially true in Canada's province of Quebec, where the use of snowshoes is firmly rooted in tradition.

One of the particularly interesting aspects of this tradition is the snowshoe club, which still has a place of honor in many parishes. The origin of these clubs apparently dates back to the time when military regiments formed teams and organized snowshoe races to whet competition and encourage physical fitness. The lineage of some of these clubs dates back more than two hundred years to early French Canadian days. Later these clubs became exclusively civilian in membership and control, but a certain touch of military esprit lingered on, as was evident in their

Nancy Kavanagh Collection

A group rabbit hunting on snowshoes near Fulton, New York, in the 1920s

continued use of drum and bugle corps, flags and banners, officers, scouts, and even mascots.

By far the most unique aspect of these snowshoe clubs was their tendency to create colorful uniforms with brightly colored sashes and knitted tuques. In the course of time, certain colors came to be identified with particular districts. For example, blue was distinctive of the area near Montreal, white around Trois-Rivières, while red was typical of Quebec itself.

Usually the color was displayed on the headgear or sashes, with the latter worn over a tunic. An arrow design often ornamented the sashes. Footgear was most often the high, soft-soled moccasin. And, of course, most important were the snowshoes, which were made especially lightweight to be swift for racing.

The English in the province of Quebec likewise were fascinated by the idea of the showshoe club and, especially in the Montreal area, founded enthusiastic organizations with many members and interesting events. Apparently the most active of all these organizations was the Montreal Snow Shoe Club founded about 1840. In 1882 its vice president, Hugh W. Becket, wrote a history and record of the club with a synopsis of the racing events of other clubs. Another excellent account of this interesting period in snowshoeing history is the article entitled "Tuque Bleue" by Rosemary Lunardini in the winter 1976 issue of *The Beaver* (published by the Hudson's Bay Co.).

In addition to arranging racing meets, these clubs also had a strong social orientation centered on the idea of good fellowship. Often during the wintertime the members would gather for an evening and hike out to an inn or tavern where they would have a good supper and then hike back, arriving at a late hour. This idea of an evening outing drifted south into the United States, as you will see in our description of the New England community snowshoe hikes. However, the strong club organization, with its races and uniforms, remained much more typical of the Canadian scene.

SNOWSHOERS' ORGANIZATIONS

On the eighth of March 1907 the Canadian Snowshoer Union was founded in the clubhouse of the Montreal Amateur Athletic Association. It aims to regulate and direct the sport of snowshoeing for about sixty member clubs located primarily in the province of Quebec. Another major purpose of the union is to maintain the customs and traditions of snowshoeing. Clubs of the union must have at least twenty-five fully active members in order to remain in good standing. From this, one can see that there are at least 1,500 enthusiastic participants in organized snowshoeing affiliated with the Canadian Snowshoer's Union.

Another organization, which was founded about 1975, is the Quebec Federation of Snowshoers and Hikers. The headquarters is in Montreal, Quebec, Canada. Provincial funds help the federation develop a trail network throughout the province and encourage its use both in summer and in winter through organized activities and programs of personal development under the heading of Sentiers-Quebec.

In 1925 the first International Snowshoe Convention was held in Lewiston, Maine; and that same year the American Snowshoer's Union was founded. This union functions in a manner similar to the Canadian Snowshoer's Union by furnishing support and guidance to slightly over twenty member clubs located in Maine, New Hampshire, Massachusetts, and Connecticut. Binding together the community of largely French-speaking interests of the Canadian and American snowshoers' unions is the International Snowshoer's Committee.

The newest on the scene is the United States Snowshoe Association (USSSA), which was organized in Corinth, New York, in 1977 and now has members in many states as well as associate members in Canada.

USSSA assists in organizing snowshoe clubs, coordinates snowshoe events, sanctions amateur snowshoe competitions, records and compiles snowshoe statistics, and encourages related industry. Furthermore, it has taken a lead in introducing a variety of new and interesting snowshoe competitions to appeal to a wide range of people.

THE OLYMPIC DREAM

There is no doubt many people across North America share a common goal of hoping to see snowshoe competitions as part of the Winter Olympic Games. Snowshoeing events are not included because snowshoeing as an athletic event is not widely practiced outside North America. There is a firm belief, however, that snowshoe competitions may soon become popular throughout the world wherever snow dominates the winter landscape. This optimism stems, in part, from the recent increase in running and racing on snowshoes here in North America. The United States Snowshoe Association sets a proposed target date of the year 2006 when you may see snowshoe exhibition events in the Winter Olympic Games in Italy. It is our fervent hope that all the snowshoe organizations will be able to work together constructively to pursue this Olympic dream!

SNOWSHOE HIKES

In reviewing the history of snowshoeing, we cannot ignore the community snowshoe hikes that were so popular in New England villages until the late 1920s and early 1930s. Reminiscences of a group in Northfield, Vermont, provide an inside look at the workings of this once very popular form of winter recreation.

Planning and organization were quite informal. At the end of any particular winter season, a group of three would take the responsibility of getting the hikes under way as soon as the snow was deep enough the following winter, usually just after the Christmas holidays. An announcement in the local newspaper invited all those who wished to assemble at a certain hour on the village square. Beforehand, the leader and his committee would have prepared a route and arranged with a farm family for refreshments. However, information concerning the route and destination was kept secret to give a sense of novelty and suspense to the tour.

The size of these groups ranged all the way from about thirty to one hundred, with an average of forty to fifty for most hikes. Old-timers and youngsters alike went along, and quite often entire families turned out for the event.

In New England, snowshoers did not have special costumes for their sport. Routine outdoor clothing, chiefly heavy wool, was worn: trousers for the men and boys, while the women and girls wore bloomers and sometimes skirts. A heavy mackinaw-type short coat kept the upper body warm and the headgear was a knitted tuque. Footgear was much the same then as now, with high moccasins and leather-

Weathering winter atop Mount Adams in New Hampshire's Presidential Range

topped pacs being preferred. In Northfield the most favored style of snowshoe was the Maine model, with the Alaskan trail or pickerel snowshoe also used sometimes. Bearpaw models were apparently not much in vogue during this period. A colorful note was struck by the women, who decorated their snowshoes with small tufts of red wool around the edge of the frames. Apparently this custom was adopted from Indians. Henri Vaillancourt, who has made extensive studies of Indian snowshoe designs, says that these decorations along the frames did, among certain tribes, show that the snowshoes were for women and children. However, in other tribes, the decorations adorned all snowshoes.

After the group had gathered, the leader would strike out at a smart pace along the planned route. The main body would then fall in line, Indian file. Stationed at the end were two skilled men who bore the peculiar title of "whippers-in." It was their responsibility to see that no one was left behind. It was also their duty to assist any floundering ladies over fences or out of the deep snow, and they usually carried along some scraps of leather and rawhide thongs should

North of Mount Rainier in Washington's Cascade Range

repairs to equipment become necessary. During the course of the march, rest stops would be made from time to time allowing the oldsters to catch their breath and the flirtatious to exchange a little flirtation.

After a couple of hours of snowshoe hiking in the brisk winter air, appetites would be whetted for the fresh-baked biscuits and homemade preserves, oyster stew, sandwiches, doughnuts, cider, and coffee that would be waiting at the destination. Group singing filled the thirty or forty minutes between the arrival of the leader and the most vigorous hikers, and that of the whippers-in. The farm family was reimbursed ten cents to twenty-five cents for the supper, depending on the situation and, no doubt, the elegance of the meal. When the hikes took place during the sugaring season it was likely that a sugar-on-snow party would be arranged, with dill pickles and raised doughnuts to accompany the sweet maple.

After supper was finished the group would reassemble for the return trip, which usually followed a different route and was planned to include, if at all possible, an open, steep, snow-covered bank down which all the hikers could slide, one snowshoe in front of the other. This part of the trip was a time for much fun and joking as some of the members tumbled head over heels down the slope when the toe of their snowshoes would catch in the snow and trip them up. Finally, the group would return to the point of departure about 10:30 or 11 P.M. and break up for the walk to their respective homes and a good night's sleep.

THE TRANSITION

At the beginning of the twentieth century, snowshoes were all constructed of natural materials—wood and animal parts—and used mostly for very utilitarian activities including hunting, trapping, expeditions, wars, and borrowing things from the neighbors. There were some snowshoe clubs in the Northeast, mostly in Canada, that snowshoed just for fun. Big changes in materials started with the use of neoprene-coated nylon instead of rawhide for lacing, lashing, and decking by the late 1950s and into the 1960s. The use of steel rods as toe cords happened in the mid-1950s, and by the mid-1960s aluminum tubing added lightness and durability to snowshoe frames.

Most of the innovative developments in materials have come since the late 1980s to the present, with the advent of plastics, composites, polyurethanes, space-age synthetics, and, of course, imagination. That imagination mixed with ingenuity increased model selections and uses. Now we have racing designs, kids' sizes, and designs specifically for women.

BIGfoot Says ▶▶

It's simple—snowshoeing really evolved to keep people from sinking up to their you-know-whats in snow while finding food or companionship, fighting, or just borrowing things from the neighbors.

Mount Rainier in Washington's Cascade Range

When the new modern Western snowshoe started to become known, then popular, some older traditional snowshoe companies shifted focus toward the new market. Until the late 1980s, only a handful of companies made them. By the mid-1990s, about two dozen companies, most with new and wonderful ideas on how to revolutionize the market, were producing snowshoes.

The guys who really started making significant changes to the old traditional wood and rawhide snowshoes were two brothers, Gene and Bill Prater, who were farmers in Ellensburg, Washington, on the east side of the Cascade Range. They were also mountain climbers, but because they were always so busy in summer raising crops, they found more time to climb in winter on snowshoes. They began experimenting with their first pairs of snowshoes in the 1950s. Both bought 10 x 56–inch Yukons with wood frames, rawhide webs, and leather bindings in 1951. Gene, who a couple of decades later authored this book, bought Lunds. Bill, who eventually started the original Sherpa Snowshoe Company, had Snowcrafts.

During the 1950s, they experimented with rawhide thongs spiral-wrapped around wood frames for traction, modified the frames by removing the tails, moved the toe cords forward and later changed to steel rods, and improved bindings and traction. In the 1960s, they started using neoprene-coated nylon for decking and straps, developed hook bindings, and used aluminum tubing for frames. They worked with snowshoe companies such as Tubbs, Snowcraft, and Lund on some of their ideas until 1971, when Bill incorporated as Sherpa Design, Inc., after the Sherpa Climbing Club, which they both belonged to. By 1973, Sherpa snowshoes were ready for market; they were first shown at the National Sporting Goods Association Sporting Goods Show in Chicago in 1974. In the late 1970s, Bill sold the company, and the Sherpa Snowshoe Company moved to Wisconsin, where it is today.

Gene continued on his own improvements, making his own but similar snowshoes under the name Prater Snowshoe Company. Gene's son, Eric, still makes some snowshoes under the family name and still operates the family farm. The Praters have been considered the originators of the "Western Mountain Snowshoe," which launched the basic design used by most companies today.

While racing in the Vail Mountain Man Winter Triathlon in 1986 and 1987, Bill Perkins, a snowshoe runner from Leadville, Colorado, was becoming dissatisfied with the full pivoting binding of the Sherpa (the main snowshoe on the racing scene at the time) because it banged him in the shins while running and it was too heavy. By the 1988 triathlon, his new improvements designed for the runner became the Redfeather Snowshoe Company, now under different ownership in Denver, Colorado. Redfeather quickly became the standard in race design with the V-tail, the fixed-hinge binding, and lightweight materials.

Tubbs Snowshoe Company from Stowe, Vermont, was founded in 1906 in Norway, Maine, by Walter F. Tubbs. The company has made traditional wood-frame snowshoes ever since and, after introducing its aluminum-frame snowshoe in 1991, has become a leader in the market through innovative management, research, and design. Its model line is extensive, with a model to fit all sizes, shapes, genders, and uses, including its asymmetrical racing design in 1993.

In 1990, Perry Kleban's graduate engineering thesis project at Stanford University became the new Atlas Snow-Shoe Company in San Francisco. While the rest of the market had been using the full pivoting toe cord and/or fixed-hinge bindings, Perry's design was spring-loaded; that, combined with other improvements in heel cleats, contoured foot beds, and durable materials, allowed Atlas to quickly become another leader in a fast-growing industry. In 1999, a major group was formed called WinterQuest, which included Tubbs, Atlas, and then Little Bear. The individual companies still operate separately while having a more solid financial position.

The snowshoe industry is continuing to grow in the United States and Canadian markets and is expanding in other countries. Many other companies are involved in the development of the industry and sport of snowshoeing. This chapter could be a whole book, but we now must move on to the equipment, accessories, and technique—the most fun uses of snow.

CHAPTER 2

Carl Heilman II / Wild Visions, Inc.

The Snowshoe

Although differences among the early snowshoe designs were likely adaptations to terrain—each shape meeting certain conditions of a local environment—difference for its own sake was probably a consideration, too, as it still is among manufacturers. Animals with feet adapted to over-snow travel provided examples: the snowshoe rabbit's hind feet inspired the shape for beavertail snowshoes and bearpaw snowshoes were modeled to resemble bobcat and lynx tracks—although bears themselves leave much deeper tracks than cats and prefer hibernation to snow travel.

The natives of Canada and Alaska brought the snowshoe to its greatest height of craftsmanship as an object of beauty as well as a useful tool for survival. The wood frames with animal hide webbing have an overall similarity, with individual differ-

◀◀ ▲ *Getting air on snowshoes*

ences. Most have one-piece frames, carefully tapered and bent to shape. Some snowshoes are works of art, with very fine lacing much too delicate to use for heavy packing in rugged mountain conditions. Perhaps these were "dress" snowshoes worn for show, much as cowboys wear "dress boots" to town.

Most **wood-frame snowshoes** are similar in design, with an outside frame and one or more wood crosspieces to help hold the shape (Figure 1). The few that do not use crosspieces have heavier, stronger frames. White ash, an eastern wood, is the choice of most manufacturers for frames; by steaming or soaking it in a special chemical bath, it can be bent without cracking and will hold the bends indefinitely. (But check for cracks before buying, and be sure both snowshoes match in size and shape.) Tightly stretched webbing, plus the weight of the wearer, tends to pull the

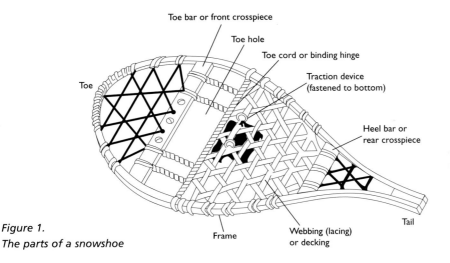

Toe bar or front crosspiece

Toe hole

Toe cord or binding hinge

Traction device
(fastened to bottom)

Toe

Heel bar or
rear crosspiece

Figure 1.
The parts of a snowshoe

Frame

Webbing (lacing)
or decking

Tail

sides of the frames together. The webbing is laced in a triangular system, with a heavily reinforced toe cord or binding hinge where the binding is attached. Lacing patterns may vary slightly, but all are basically similar. Thicker, heavier lacing is used for the section under the foot than for the toe and tail parts. Lacing used in colder areas where there is consistent powder snow is thinner than that used south of the U.S.-Canadian border where the wetter snow rapidly destroys lightweight lacing.

Traditionally, wood-frame snowshoes have been manufactured in the eastern United

States and in Quebec, Canada. During World War II the demand for snowshoes apparently increased; many military surplus webs show trademarks from Michigan and Arkansas as well as the eastern states.

Now, practically all wood-frame snowshoes are made in the Snow Belt from Minnesota to the northeastern United States and north into eastern Canada. Metal-frame models were developed almost entirely in mountains near the West Coast, but are now made in the most unlikely places from coast to coast.

BASIC TYPES

For simplicity, I classify snowshoe types into five basic categories: Yukon, Ojibwa, beavertail, bearpaw, and Western (Figure 2). Sizes overlap and regional names are profuse and contradictory, but for general purposes the five-design description is adequate.

The **Yukon** can range from about 10 to 11 inches wide and from 42 to 62 inches in length. Most have a very high toe turnup, to 6 or 8 inches. Traditionally, these are best in open country and deep powder snow. The narrow width also makes them good for traversing slopes and the best type for descending steep slopes in soft snow. Their high toes ride up out of the snow and seldom catch on anything. However, the over-50-inch length and heavy weight make Yukons unwieldy for maneuvering in tight quarters, and the high toe can't be kicked into the snow to climb (step kicking), so these are not for mountain travel. This

design is also called the Alaskan, Pickerel, or Cross Country.

The **Ojibwa,** like the Yukon, is long and narrow, except that it is pointed at the tip as well as at the tail. The use is also similar; however, the pointed tip cuts through thick brush and deep snow with less piling of snow on the tips. Instead of a one-piece frame bent around 180 degrees at the tip and attached at the tail, the Ojibwa frame is made with two separate curved sides attached at both ends. Ojibwa widths can range from 9 to 12 inches with lengths from 36 to 60 inches.

The **beavertail** has such local names as Maine, Michigan, and Huron. Widths have been from 10 inches to as wide as 20 inches and lengths from 30 to 48 inches. Generally, they are almost flat, or with a maximum toe rise of only 3 inches, and have a long tail. The flatter toes make these the best for step kicking, and they are the favorite with eastern climbers for use in tough snowshoeing conditions. Widths of 12 inches and over are poor for sidehilling (traveling across a slope) but give the desired flotation in powder snow. The trade-off is often worth it, since snowshoers in the East seem to go straight up hills much more often than across them. Despite the width, beavertails have an overlapping pattern on the trail (Figure 2), which is helpful when following a trailbreaker who is wearing narrower snowshoes.

Bearpaws, as the name implies, are short and wide, with rounded tails. Sizes range from 12 to 19 inches in width and from 24 to 33 inches in length. The most

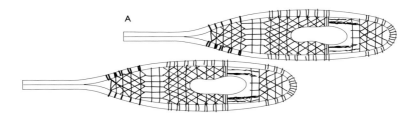

Figure 2.
The types of snowshoes

   A.   Yukon
   B.   Ojibwa
   C.   Beavertail
   D.   Bearpaw
   E.   Western

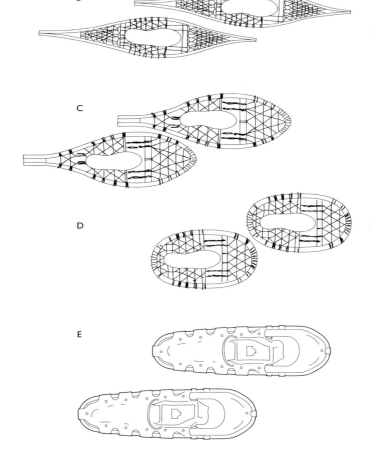

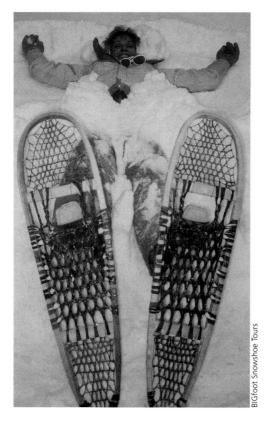

Modified bearpaw, Green Mountain style

Molded plastic on snowshoes

New modern Western snowshoes, kids' style

common sizes are probably 13 or
14 inches wide by 29 to 33 inches long.
Thus they are rather rounded and usually
flat, which makes them one of the best for
kicking steps. The shorter length ensures
easy maneuvering, although a width of
12 inches and over is a drawback on
sidehills or squeezing between trees.

The flat toes of bearpaws will run under
the surface during a steep descent, although
lengths of 28 inches or shorter may be
"heeled in" to kick steps on the way down.
This can be a great advantage when you are
descending very steep slopes in powder
snow and can counteract the tendency of the
flat toes to run under and trip you. Some
people feel the rounded tails cause more
drag than a snowshoe with a narrow, pointed
tail; however, drag on a slippery surface
should be minimal. Lacing at the rear must

32

be reinforced heavily because it abrades rapidly on a hard crust or in wet spring snow that has many sharp ice crystals in it.

The **modified bearpaw,** Green Mountain style (see photo on page 32), seems to have been developed to compensate for the shortcomings of the original bearpaw. It is narrower, usually 9 to 11 inches, and not as round, with lengths up to 40 inches (a very common size being 10 x 36 inches), giving even more manueverability in the mountains. Instead of having flat toes, a slight rise of about 3 to 4 inches keeps one from toeing into the snow and tripping as often. This multi-modified design might be considered the precursor to the modern Western snowshoe—sort of a wood Western or premodern.

First developed in the 1950s, **Western** snowshoes (see photo on page 32) were modified in the 1970s and since have become a favorite with many snowshoers. They are generally smaller than wood-framed snowshoes, usually with a high toe turnup and a short toe section, made with aluminum frames and a synthetic decking that is laced or riveted to the frame and replaces the lacing (webbing). Sizes typically range from 8 by 22 inches to 10 by 36 inches. The frames are made mostly of aluminum tubing, but some have been of angle or I-beam aluminum. While most are symmetrical in shape, some designs use asymmetrical patterns for specialty and racing models. The only crosspiece is usually combined with a binding hinge, which functions as the toe cord on laced snowshoes. This binding hinge provides precise control of the snowshoe, allowing almost no lateral slack between the boot and the snowshoe. A cleat or claw is attached to the underside of this crosspiece to increase traction.

At present, all models of Western snowshoes have factory-equipped bindings that are bolted or riveted to the snowshoe and are not interchangeable with other Western bindings. In one type of design, a metal pivot hinge is attached to the frame with wide neoprene straps. This allows some flex or give, taking some strain off the frames and allowing the traction device to sink more deeply into the snow than devices on snowshoes with a more rigid crosspiece. (For more on bindings, see Chapter 3.)

Western snowshoes were designed in the West for mountain use. Their light weight and excellent binding and traction have combined to give outstanding maneuverability, and the high toe is a real asset in soft snow. This style is now the most popular snowshoe, not only in the West but also throughout the U.S. and Canadian Snow Belt and around the world. Western snowshoes have their greatest advantage in soft but firm snow like that found in the coastal mountains of the West and late winter snow found elsewhere. The claws make them very adaptable to icy conditions. Obviously, the smaller sizes will not provide adequate flotation in powder snow, except for lighter people, but the larger sizes will do the job.

Plastic snowshoes have gone through many developments in materials, inclusions within the molds for strength and attachments, designs with built-in traction, and colors to catch the eye. In the past they have not been too well received as a heavy-duty, backcountry snowshoe, but they are making progress. Their greatest popularity has been for gentler hikes, for timber surveying, for use as emergency equipment on snowmobiles, and for general recreational use. Generally they are lightweight, lower priced than most metal-frame snowshoes, and have a waxy surface that lessens the ability of snow to freeze on or stick to them as it does to wood and metal. Some early models were too flexible, and the plastic used in others fatigued and eventually broke. Research is overcoming those problems. The manufacturing processes are often referred to as injection-molded or rim-molded (when molded around a frame). The shapes and sizes vary from the standard Western configurations to many other imaginative concepts.

Refer to Chart 1 ("Traditional Wood Frames") and Chart 2 ("Modern Metal Frames") for shape and size comparisons.

CHARACTERISTICS

The basic shape of a snowshoe affects its handling characteristics. For example, the action of the snowshoe tail dragging on the snow and the toe rising in the air as the shoe is lifted is called tracking. A snowshoe with a long toe and a short, light tail does not track well; the toe often catches under deep snow or crust and must be wrenched free to prevent a fall. You should be able to simply lift each foot and shove it forward, knowing

that the snowshoe will follow precisely. One 10 x 36–inch model with special forward-mounted toe cord tracks very well, in spite of its short length, as do the 8-inch-wide short, metal-frame snowshoes.

Long Yukon 10 x 56–inch models track well, and their high toes seldom catch under the snow. Bearpaws do not track as well, and the toes often catch. Most short wood-frame snowshoes have such light tails that a relatively small weight of snow on the toe will cause it to catch, so that the tail rather than the toe rises as you step forward.

Some beavertails seem to suffer from the same design weakness as the bearpaw: the toes are too long in relation to the tail. On level trails this tendency is not too noticeable, but when climbing, traversing, or descending, the wide, long toe section frequently runs under the snow and must be wrenched free to prevent a fall.

A snowshoe's traction depends on its webbing and crossbars biting into the snow, and some designs have better natural traction than others. The location of the toe cord in relation to the front of the snowshoe is vital. Placing the toe cord one-fourth of the length of the snowshoe from the toe improves traction by placing weight well forward, causing the toe to dig in deeper than on a snowshoe that supports weight nearer the tail. Figure 3 shows that the forward-mounted toe cord or binding hinge causes the snowshoe to almost make its own step as you climb a slope. On short snowshoes this has another advantage. The 10 x 36–inch standard snowshoe, for example, has such a long, nearly flat toe that

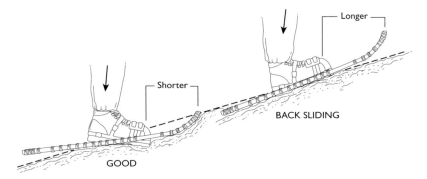

Figure 3. Location of toe cord and foot position in relation to front of snowshoe. Left is good—foot is forward, toe digs in, platform is more level, traction is good. Right is bad—foot is too far back, tail digs in, platform is steeply angled, traction is weak.

it frequently catches, tripping the snowshoer (Figure 4). The forward toe cord changes the proportions of the 10 x 36–inch model so that the toe does not catch, except possibly when descending. The weight of the tail section overbalances almost any load of snow the toe may gather when climbing.

Short, flat snowshoes with the forward toe cord do have this one weakness. When plunge-stepping—that is, taking long, stiff-kneed steps—downhill in soft snow, the toes dig in deeper than the tails. In this situation the toes can catch and cause a fall, especially if the snow is crusty. Using a snowshoe with at least a 3- or 4-inch toe turnup minimizes or eliminates the problem.

Even on easy snowshoe hikes there is a certain amount of scrambling over or around obstructions that is neither climbing nor sidehilling. In the real backcountry this type of travel may predominate, with infrequent easy places.

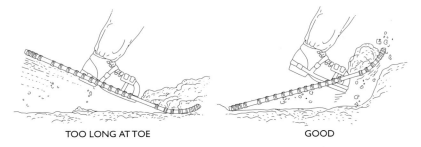

TOO LONG AT TOE   GOOD

Figure 4. Effect of length of toe. Left, short snowshoe with long toe catches under the snow easily; right, very short toe does not catch under the snow easily.

35

On such terrain a small, lightweight, maneuverable snowshoe with good tracking ability gives a real advantage.

The advantages of the 8 x 25 and 9 x 30 Western designs are their light weight, small size, ease of handling, and superb traction. Snowshoeing with these small snowshoes is an extension of bare-boot walking or scrambling, but on firm, hard snow. The small Western or a small bearpaw make it possible to do this type of scrambling on snow that is too soft for bare-boot travel in much of the winter, though these snowshoes are not as practical for deep, loose new snow that hasn't firmed up.

It is possible for a snowshoe to sidehill and climb better than anyone else's, yet be so heavy and cumbersome that even a short hike is exhausting. Although the trend in snowshoes has been toward small, narrow, lightweight models, some manufacturers still ignore this critical factor.

As the British planned their 1953 Mount Everest expedition, it was calculated that one pound on the foot was as fatiguing as five pounds carried on the back, primarily because the distant end of the leg is an awkward and tiring place to carry extra weight. A 10 x 56–inch snowshoe with deluxe traction and binding can weigh six to seven pounds. A small Western snowshoe weighs less than two pounds. The extra eight pounds per pair of 10 x 56–inch snowshoes is the equivalent of forty extra pounds in the pack.

Snowshoeing is tiring when compared with hiking in boots on a dry trail, and long, heavy snowshoes are exhausting unless you are conditioned to the extra weight. Small, light snowshoes, sufficient for support, will get you farther for equivalent effort.

Snowshoes may seem weightless compared with downhill skis, boots, and bindings. But when attempting to make turns on an uphill pull, it is a different story, especially for the lead person breaking trail through deep, heavy snow with its extra weight on the webs. And if you are on an overnight trip and have forty or more pounds in your pack, you will appreciate the truth of the Everest formula.

BIGfoot Says ▶▶

Bigger is not always better when selecting snowshoes. Consider your use, total weight with pack, and snow conditions. Remember the Mount Everest rule: one pound on the foot equals five pounds in the pack. Think smaller and lighter unless you are going heavy and deeper. And use double poles to help offset the added weight of larger, heavier snowshoes.

LACING

Traditional snowshoe lacing material is raw, not tanned, cowhide. The heaviest lacing available is necessary for mountain use. Two things put it to the test: moisture and abrasion. Rocks and other objects sticking through the snow, or thinly veiled by a layer of powder that hides but does not shield, can be a third, cutting the cord the same way edges of potholes abrade car tires.

Rawhide is the first choice for a lacing that can survive abrasion and rock-cut damage in subfreezing temperatures. It is nearly indestructible as long as it stays cold. However, at temperatures above 30°F rawhide becomes soaked and loses about half its strength. When wet it stretches easily and loses much of its abrasion resistance.

Neoprene-covered nylon is a better lacing choice for use in wet snow, rating well above rawhide. Though wet spring snow above 30°F has sharp ice crystals that abrade both kinds of lace, neoprene lasts longer in such conditions than wet rawhide. Neoprene also exceeds rawhide's ability to resist rock cuts at these temperatures.

Rock cuts may seem a minor hazard in the West, where there is supposed to be plenty of snow to cover such problems. But there are windswept ridges and plenty of downed conifers. Conifers have lots of branches and they seem to break with sharp ends. These sharp tips are certainly a hazard, especially in logged areas.

The East is where snowshoes take the worst beating in the North American Snow Belt. The area near and above tree line is so wind-blasted that it usually seems to be more rock than snow. Trails are amazingly rocky, too, and steep sections, which are the majority of the trails, have granite clinkers the size of footballs covered with knife-pointed quartz crystals strewn liberally under a thin layer of powder snow. Choose heavy-duty lacing to snowshoe in these areas.

The greatest weakness of neoprene lacing is probably quality control at the factory. When manufactured properly, the neoprene is firmly bonded to the nylon fiber that provides its strength. The nylon is very strong but wears out rapidly when rubbing on snow if the neoprene separates from it, and it abrades rapidly when wrapped around metal, even faster than when wrapped around wood.

Polyurethane was the next lacing material introduced on Western snowshoes. It rates better than either rawhide or neoprene in abrasion resistance and like neoprene does not absorb water. It has great elasticity, which is one of its greatest assets. Under strain it is more likely to stretch and spring back than to break either the lace or the frame.

Polyurethane ranks poorest of these three materials in resistance to cutting. Rocks knife through it because it contains no fiber, unlike neoprene lace; a nick may in time cause a break. Part of the problem is the metal frame, which the lace wraps around, because it is harder than wood. When the lace is pinched between a rock and the tubing, the lace may be severed. If you are going to snowshoe in an area with windswept, rocky ridges, look for the heaviest lace available.

Nylon cord has also been used for lacing. It must be protected from abrasion since it does not survive well on rough crust or wet snow. In an effort to offer protection, one manufacturer uses an epoxy coating on eighth-inch cord, and another maker has a varnish dip on quarter-inch rope. Nylon cord is not used on very many models.

The most visible difference between the Western snowshoe and the wood-frame snowshoe is the Western's use of synthetic decking, which takes the place of traditional webbing. Neoprene-covered nylon was originally the most common decking material. Most manufacturers now use various types of plastics or heavy custom fabrics, which are wrapped around the frames at strategic points and riveted instead of laced.

The waxy surface of the synthetic decking sheds snow better than webbing, permitting snow to slide off the snowshoe, an advantage when you're breaking trail. However, decking is extremely slippery, unlike webbing, which bites into the snow. As a result, all snowshoes with synthetic decking have to be equipped with adequate traction devices to be effective.

Once in a while someone compares decking with webbing and concludes that the webbing, with all those openings, provides less flotation than decking. However, snow doesn't slide through small openings well at all. In a laboratory using precise test equipment, a difference might be detected, but on the trail, any difference in flotation is imperceptible, even to the fussiest snowshoer.

CHOOSING A SNOWSHOE

Frame design, webbing or decking, tracking, toe turnup, size, and weight all affect choice of snowshoe. Every design has some disadvantages. A compromise must be made when buying, because no design solves all problems for all people in all places. And sometimes people as independently minded as snowshoers pick their snowshoe because they like a certain shape or material, even though the "experts" recommend something else. If you want to go snowshoeing somewhere, almost any kind will get you there if you are determined enough.

Most places have a certain type of snowshoe that is traditionally used in the local area. Given the initial choices of wood, metal, or molded as well as the variety of sizes and shapes, in addition to determining whether they're for occasional use, for the backcountry, or for running, along with a salesperson's suggestions and the manufacturer's recommendations, making a decision can be quite overwhelming. Only a few shops across the country have a large choice of models and sizes, while most do their best to stock what works for their area. Although I haven't snowshoed in every snowy area in North America, I have some suggestions to help beginners.

LOCATION

Different geographical areas have quite different requirements for snowshoes. For example, in the western coastal ranges where "warm" winter temperatures cause the snow to firm up quickly, small Western snowshoes work very well. Often a 200-pound person will be quite happy with the smallest size, although most people prefer more flotation.

The interior of British Columbia; the Rockies of Montana, Wyoming, and Colorado; the Wasatch of Utah; and the Sierra of California are a great deal colder than the Cascades of Washington and Oregon. Snow is fluffier, so a larger snowshoe is required for flotation, that is until the snow firms up later in the season.

SNOWSHOE LENGTH
AND SNOW CONDITIONS

Wherever you snowshoe, you will hear of some person who traveled great distances on immense snowshoes while sinking knee-deep or more in bottomless powder snow. Any of the mountain areas mentioned can have 24 to 36 inches or more of snowfall overnight, and 8 to 10 feet or more if a storm lasts several days. Few recreational snowshoers travel very far under such conditions, unless they are caught back in the hills by a storm and must get out in a given time. Old-timers have a tendency to sneer at present-day short, narrow, light-weight snowshoes that obviously will sink out of sight in the fluff deposited by such a storm. It takes a snowshoe like an extra-large Yukon or bearpaw to travel in really soft snow. Actually, this kind of major storm is rather infrequent. The old tradition of iron men on big snowshoes is being put to rest. It is less exhausting to wait a few days for new snow to firm up and then use smaller lightweight equipment. It also is safer in avalanche country to wait a few days and let the slides run, too.

If you are carrying a heavy pack and sinking 12 inches in powder snow on giant snowshoes, you may travel only a few miles in rough country in a hard day. Sinking in 18 inches or more, which is about knee-deep, you may measure the distance traveled in yards rather than miles. So, especially in mountain country, snowshoers are waiting for firm snow and replacing their large heavy snowshoes with smaller lightweight models. Snow travel is so much easier on firm snow than on the bottomless variety that waiting a few days is well worth it.

A mountain guide who climbs in British Columbia's Purcell Mountains in winter advises that if you can't kick steps with your snowshoe, it's no good in the mountains. This is good advice, and if the snowshoe is over 3 feet long, it's too unwieldy for mountain use.

Easterners agree. However, step kicking in the eastern mountains is probably more severe than in any other area of North America. Typically, there is a crust on the snow there. Snowshoes should have nearly flat toes that can really be bashed into the crust to make a step.

This technique may leave most of the snowshoe sticking out in the air, whereas in soft western snow—either wet and sloppy or powder—the snowshoe is rather casually stomped down to make a deep step with only the tail sticking out. The difference in surfaces has led to two very different styles of kicking steps and different snowshoes best adapted to these techniques. As one is definitely used in the East and the other in

A steep pitch en route to the summit of Cannon Mountain, New Hampshire

the West, I use the terms eastern technique and western technique. (See more in Chapter 8, "Walking on Snowshoes.")

There are many more Western snowshoes with high toes—3 to 6 inches of toe rise—in use in the coastal mountains of the West than there are flat beavertails and bearpaws. The Western snowshoe is becoming a popular choice in New England, too, although there are a lot of wood snowshoes still used in this area.

Comfort on descents also has a bearing on whether to choose flatter or higher toes. Most western mountains have softer snow throughout the winter, seldom crusting as

the eastern mountains do after a January thaw. So descents are generally in soft snow, where a higher toe helps keep the snowshoe from running under the snow and tripping the snowshoer.

CLIMBING ABILITY

In addition to easterners, another category of snowshoers usually puts climbing ability as the highest priority for snowshoe choice after size. These are people who work on steep, timbered slopes in winter, surveying or marking trees for logging. They often follow compass lines, section lines, or other routes that must be followed as precisely as possible no matter how rugged the terrain is. Deep gullies must be crossed and steep hills ascended while in the line of duty.

The emphasis so far has been on snowshoes for mountain country. The problems created by steep slopes and hard snow are best solved by fairly small snowshoes that can be placed very accurately just where you want them. For more gentle terrain, the main concern is to have enough flotation without excessive weight. The larger the snowshoe, the less you sink in soft snow. The shape may be long and narrow or short and wide.

One way to see for yourself which snowshoe has the larger surface (thus more flotation) is to place one on top of another and estimate how much bigger it is by comparing the actual flotation surface. Remember, that surface does not include a long skinny tail or a very high toe rise, which doesn't add much flotation at all.

The differences in wood-frame shapes and sizes sometimes are not that different in flotation ability.

A second comparison to make is between the size of the snowshoer and the snowshoe itself. A 5-foot-long snowshoe is not suited for a very short person. A strapping 6-foot, 4-inch athlete can cover a lot of miles on large, heavy snowshoes without excessive fatigue, but small women, middle-aged or sedentary persons, and young teenagers probably don't have the stamina to do this. Thus a person's dimensions should be matched to the snowshoe.

After making the above comparisons, the third and ultimate way to help select a style is to try the snowshoes on the snow. Many retail shops, manufacturers, and local clubs have demonstration days and snowshoe festivals to introduce potential buyers to the sport. If nature cooperates, you can try different sizes and types on firm snow, in powder, and on some hillsides. Or try renting before you buy; some shops will even apply rental costs to the purchase price.

Also, keep in mind that a wide snowshoe forces a person to walk with the feet wide apart (Figure 5). To hold the feet apart so a wide snowshoe doesn't bump you on the opposite ankle or calf is tiring to the tendons on the outside of each hip joint. A first-time snowshoer or very small person on wide, heavy snowshoes is often surprised at the new pain from this exertion, termed "ball joint fatigue." The 8- to 9-inch-wide Westerns aren't as likely to cause a problem as the wider wood-frame versions.

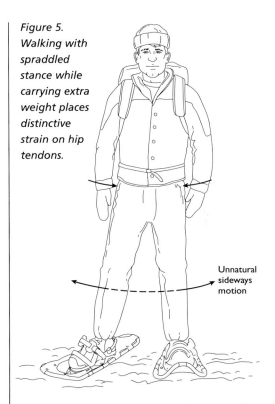

Figure 5. Walking with spraddled stance while carrying extra weight places distinctive strain on hip tendons.

Unnatural sideways motion

Choose a snowshoe that will work well in a variety of conditions. In general, all through the Snow Belt, you will find the softest, deepest powder snow in December and January. In February it will be firming

BIGfoot Says ▶▶
Modern snowshoe manufacturers are adding models for smaller folks and adjusting for the differences in stride by tapering the frame width to a narrower tail. Some flotation surface is lost; however, stride comfort is gained.

CHART 1: TRADITIONAL WOOD FRAMES

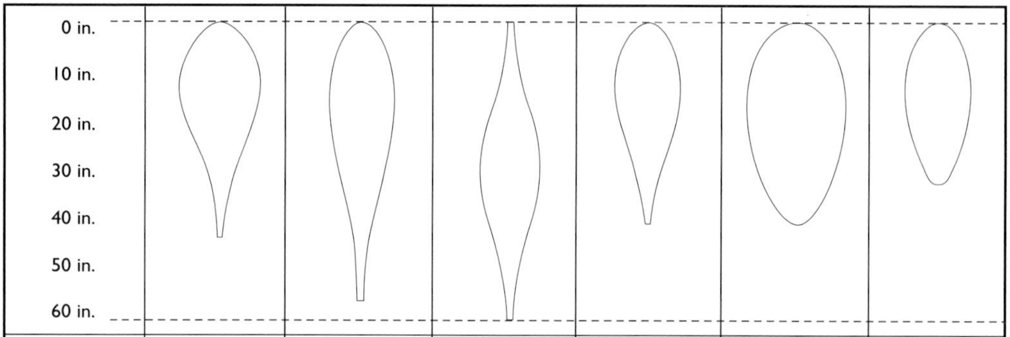

	0 in. — 60 in. (shapes)					
SHAPE NAMES (generic)	• Huron • Michigan • Maine (Beavertail)	• Alaskan • Yukon • Pickerel • Cross Country	• Ojibwa • Cree	• Modified Bearpaw • Westover	• Bearpaw	• Modified Bearpaw, • Green Mountain • Appalachian
SMALL most-used sizes	10 × 33 12 × 42 12 × 46	10 × 46	9 × 36 10 × 48	7 × 30 10 × 48	13 × 29	9 × 28 10 × 30
weight range	up to 220 lbs	up to 200 lbs	up to 130 lbs	up to 160 lbs	up to 150 lbs	up to 170 lbs
MEDIUM most-used sizes	13 × 46	11 × 46	11 × 54	11 × 32 12 × 35	14 × 30 13 × 33	10 × 35 13 × 36
weight range	150 to 240 lbs	140 to 215 lbs	130 to 200 lbs	140 to 200 lbs	up to 150 lbs	150 to 225 lbs
LARGE most-used sizes	14 × 46 14 × 48	10 × 56 11 × 56	12 × 60	13 × 35 14 × 35		11 × 40
weight range	175+ lbs	175+ lbs	175+ lbs	up to 250 lbs		175+ lbs
TIP RISE	+/- 3"	+/- 8" (+/- 4")	+/- 8"	+/- 3"	Flat to slight rise	+/- 3" to 4"
BEST GENERAL USE	• Deep snow • Rolling terrain	• Deep snow • Open terrain	• Rolling terrain • Brush and bushes	• Moderate terrain	• Deep snow when maneuverability is needed	• Mountainous terrain • Firmer snow

up, and in March and April you will find firm snow. Heavy snowfalls in late winter firm up faster than in January. The farther north you are, the later these stages occur. However, winter weather is so unpredictable that there may be a lot more variety in snow conditions than you might expect.

I have used a great many sizes and shapes of snowshoes, on various terrains and types of snow. Over the years I have experimented with a lot of gimmicks as well as accepted designs and have ended up handcrafting my own snowshoes. For powder snow in early winter I use a 7 1/2 x 40–inch Western-type snowshoe. For firm

CHART 2: MODERN METAL FRAMES (may include plastic rim or injection molded)

BASIC SHAPES		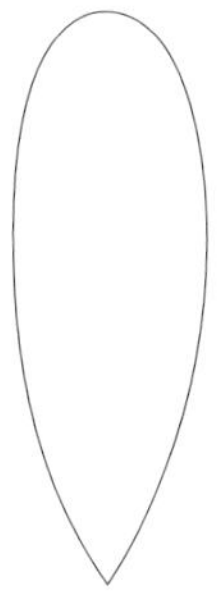	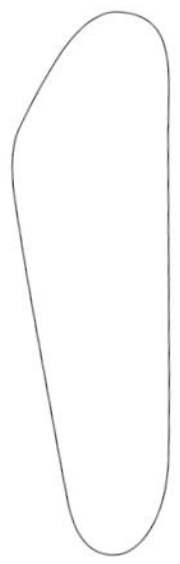	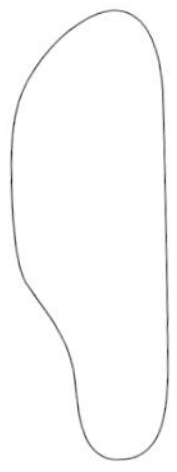	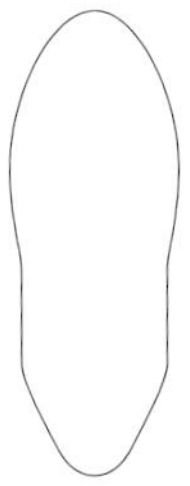
Symmetrical	X	X			X
Asymmetrical			X	X	
VARIATIONS OF SHAPES ABOVE	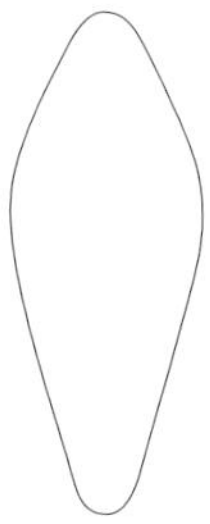		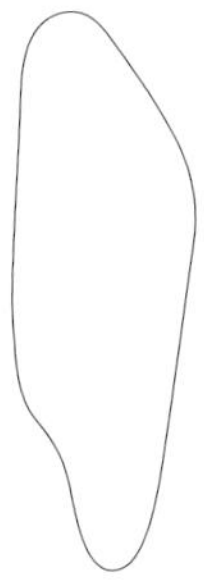		
SMALL • small folks • mountains • firm snow • fitness/jogging	8 × 21 8 × 22 8 × 25 8 × 26	8 × 22 8 × 25	7 × 24 8 × 25	8 × 25	8 × 24 8 × 25
	*WEIGHT RANGE: 100 lbs to 200 lbs (including pack) ☆				
MEDIUM • powder for small folks • firm snow for large folks • mountains • deep powder	8 × 30 9 × 27 9 × 30	9 × 29 9 × 30 9 × 33	8 × 28 9 × 30	8 × 30	8 × 26 8 × 30 9 × 28
	*WEIGHT RANGE: 140 lbs to 250 lbs (including pack) ☆				
LARGE • larger folks • deeper powder • rolling hills	8 × 36 10 × 36 9 × 34 8 × 34	10 × 34 10 × 36	9 × 32		10 × 29 10 × 30
	*WEIGHT RANGE: 160 lbs to 275 lbs (including pack) ☆				
X-LARGE • big folks • heavy loads	10 × 37 11 × 38	10 × 42			
	*WEIGHT RANGE: 200 lbs and above (including pack) ☆				
RACERS	8 × 25	8 × 22 8 × 25	7 × 24	8 × 25	
TIP RISE	From 3 to 6 inches or slightly above				

* For general all-around use, choose smaller shoes rather than larger.
☆ Weights are averages of manufacturers' suggestions considering snow conditions.

snow, such as late winter in the Cascades and spring in colder ranges, a 7 ½ x 30–inch design is adequate. There are times when it is less fatiguing to sink a little deeper with a small snowshoe that handles easily than fight a big, heavy snowshoe.

When using wood-frame snowshoes, if the route doesn't climb steeply and the snow is exceedingly deep and soft, a good choice would be a medium to large Ojibwa, with pointed toe and tail and a toe rise of 6 to 8 inches. If the route has steep descending slopes in this same deep powder, a Yukon would be better, except that they don't climb steep slopes well. If steep is going to be the game, a medium to large modified bearpaw—Green Mountain, for example—would work well since it will handle a traverse.

And whether it's level country or mountain, I'd rather be patient and wait for good traveling conditions so I can use a small, lightweight snowshoe instead of

BIGfoot Says ▸▸

Although modern snowshoes don't often break in the wild, if rivets pop out of the decking wrapped to the frame, looping cable ties twice around through the holes is a good temporary fix. For a binding repair, carry about 80 inches of ½- to ¾-inch-wide nylon webbing strap with a buckle at one end and use it to make an emergency Lampwick binding (Figure 13) or some creative alternative, which will get you back to the trailhead. Be sure to practice at home!

larger ones. If you are going snowshoeing in gentle country, you don't need all that heavy equipment designed for mountains. But, after all these suggestions, recommendations, and guidelines, in the final analysis it is your judgment and a personal choice to balance flotation and weight against lightness and maneuverability.

Most manufacturers rate their snowshoes for weight of person and type of snow. I would suggest using their recommendations as much as possible and add local preference. I have tried to simplify the different manufacturers' recommendations with averages in groups of small, medium, and large—with extra-large for metal frames only. Refer to Chart 1, "Traditional Wood Frames," and Chart 2, "Modern Metal Frames," which show that the weight ranges overlap between sizes. The sizes shown are only those that are popular among the major manufacturers; there may be other dimensions made in your locale, especially with the wood-frame snowshoes. When picking your weight range, don't forget to allow for a heavy pack, if you are going to use one. For general all-around use, choose the smaller size rather than the larger. Then go out and have fun!

MAINTENANCE AND REPAIR

Wood frames and rawhide need routine maintenance. Clear spar varnish or shellac is the traditional material, although some people prefer more color, and paint is nearly as durable as varnish. Polyurethane coatings are becoming very popular and are quite durable. Whenever the finish wears off the wood, it's time to get out the brush and redo the snowshoe. The same rule of thumb applies to the rawhide. Powder snow is not very abrasive and in cold temperatures there is very little wear on the bottoms of snowshoes. In wet snow the story is different, since rawhide soon gets soaked and varnish starts flaking off. Most of us have seen snowshoes with the rawhide bleached out and wear showing on the frames. The hard part of the wood grain stands out because softer wood fibers have been worn away.

A special Cascade Mountain recipe for early-1900s "Snowshoe Dope" comes from Morris Jenkins of Cle Elum, Washington, who trapped and cruised timber on snowshoes for years. The special ingredient is pitch from a fir tree. This must be of thin-syrup consistency and can come from two sources. One is an old-growth tree with a "wind-shook" seam, where a living tree has a split that is still dripping pitch after it has been felled during logging. Sometimes a gallon may be collected from one tree of this type. The second source is pitch blisters on a growing tree, but this is a much messier job and takes longer to collect.

For those of you who actually have access to either such tree, the dope is eight parts clear shellac, two parts pitch, and one part beeswax (paraffin). Heat and mix thoroughly, but do not boil. Warm the snowshoe to room temperature. Use a small paintbrush and paint the frames,

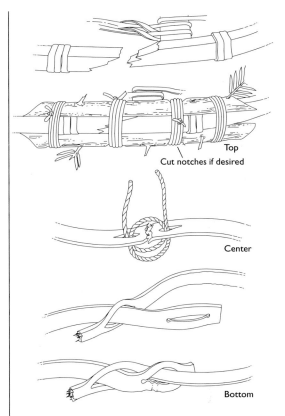

Figure 6. (Top) Repairing a broken frame with a splint of branches. Four wraps of cord will hold it in place.

(Center) Splice for broken strap or webbing. Cut slit in ends near break, thread cord through, pull tight, and tie.

(Bottom) Splicing a broken strap. First slip split end of severed section onto either piece. Then slip loose end of severed section through hole of other piece, and pull tight.

45

lacing, and binding with the dope. This will waterproof and protect even in wet snow since it doesn't dry brittle but stays flexible. Two dopings per winter should be sufficient for heavy use in coastal slush; however, more applications may be necessary if wear removes the earlier coating. Do not dry a snowshoe near a hot fire because it can damage rawhide, neoprene, polyurethane, and wood frames.

Neoprene lace is a no-maintenance material, but if it gets "hairy," as described earlier, it may be a good idea to give it a haircut. Some jogging shoe repair cement will prolong life if the lacing gets worn under your boot heel—a place of considerable abrasion—or where a rock has snagged it so the nylon fibers show.

The metal-frame and synthetic-decking snowshoes are advertised as no-maintenance. This is fairly accurate. However, the need to varnish wood snowshoes makes it imperative to examine them minutely several times each winter. This way you pick up any nearly broken webbing or other problems. Check over no-maintenance "webs" periodically. It's better to find and repair problems at home, where tools are available and the work can be done at a comfortable temperature. It can be almost overwhelming to discover that your snowshoes are falling apart after dark, in a blizzard, several miles from your car.

The variety of slopes and snow conditions in hill or mountain country tends to present situations that are harder on snowshoes than those presented in open country. The main cause of a broken frame is stepping on a hole or depression in such a way that the toe

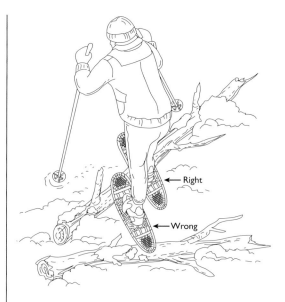

Figure 7. *The wrong* way to step over logs, branches, depressions, or holes is to "bridge" the obstacle with weight on the snowshoe toe and tail. The *right* way is to place weight on the ball-of-foot claw, stepping on the log or high point, or find a better route around the obstacle.

and tail of the shoe are on higher points than the middle of the foot, with perhaps the middle 24 inches of frame **bridging** the hole (see Figure 7). Often, ridge tops are blown free of snow, revealing sharp rocks and frozen clods, which can cut webbing and damage frames. There are many obstructions that can be lightly covered by snow, such as fallen trees, branches, and rocks. A gentle step may do no more than scratch the frame, but jumping off something may create enough force to break the frame or cut the webbing. (Snowshoers seem to delight in jumping off things [see photo on page 26] because the soft landing is so different from crashing down on bare ground.) But stepping into small depressions; jumping onto hard, hummocky snow; wading rocky streambeds; and falling into tree holes are the most common maneuvers that damage snowshoes.

First aid for a broken frame is the same as for a broken bone. In forested country, cut a couple of small branches to use as splints; lay one on top and one under the break, and wrap tightly with $\frac{1}{8}$-inch nylon cord (Figure 6). This will last quite well, especially since the snowshoer will then be much more careful of the footgear.

Incidentally, frame breakage has not been a problem with metal frames. However, any frame that is accidentally bent while snowshoeing will break completely if straightened. An emergency field repair is the same splint used to repair a broken wooden snowshoe. Carry plenty of $\frac{1}{8}$-inch nylon cord for repairs, no matter what kind of snowshoe you are using. And hope there is a convenient branch to provide the splint. Plastic cable ties can also be used instead of nylon cord for emergency repairs.

Broken rawhide and neoprene webbing are spliced the same way. Make a lengthwise split in the ends, thread the repair cord through, tighten, and tie off. It is hard to do a neat job of this with either a knife blade or leather punch without a lot of practice. It is easy, however, to slice straps and laces when the knife slips, and with the same stroke slice through good webbing and end up with the knife point stuck in your hand. To prevent this "great downward slash," place the webbing or strap on the frame of your wood snowshoe—or on any available stick—press down firmly, and use several strokes of your recently sharpened knife to make the cut. Wet rawhide is exceedingly slimy and snaky, and it has a tendency to roll over when you are making cuts.

Repairing cut polyurethane lace is difficult in the field and happens too seldom to suggest that the clips and pliers used by the manufacturer be carried in one's repair kit. It is practically impossible to tie anything to this slippery, flexible material. However, unrepaired lace can unravel along quite a length of snowshoe. Carry nylon cord, cable ties, or plastic heavy-duty electrical wire ties to hold things together until you get back home, where more permanent repairs can be made.

For broken nylon cord it is best to tie loops in the broken ends, thread repair cord through the loops, and tie off the cord. Knots in nylon have a tendency to come untied unless you really tighten them down—even then you can't trust them.

I have used the word "Western" as a design or type, because these snowshoes are so different from wood-frame laced models. Years ago the first Western snowshoe sold throughout the Snow Belt was manufactured in Washington State. But the name doesn't fit geographically any more. The former Washington-made Western is now made in Wisconsin, with other Westerns made in California, Utah, Colorado, and as far east as Vermont, with various others in between. My few pairs of handmade Westerns are still made in Washington.

CHAPTER 3

Bindings

The second vital part of the basic snowshoe package is the binding, which must make a positive connection between the foot and the snowshoe. To allow comfortable walking, the binding must hinge freely, the heel rising as the boot toe goes into the toe hole (Figure 8). Any restriction on the hinging movement will limit a comfortable stride. If the binding or boot hits the side of the toe hole or catches on the toe bar, it may cause the snowshoe toe to dig in and trip the wearer. The binding should be easily adjustable, so that any such problem can be quickly remedied.

The binding should strictly limit the hinging action to up and down motion, gripping the boot tightly so there is practically no lateral movement. When the foot

◀◀ ▲ *Snowshoeing off the summit of Telescope Peak. California's Death Valley is in the distance.*

turns left or right, the snowshoe should turn precisely the same way, with preferably less than an inch of sideways movement at the boot heel on wood snowshoes and no such lateral movement on Westerns (the precise binding hinge prevents it). When the snowshoe responds this positively, it is possible to move confidently through rough terrain without tripping on obstacles and slipping on sidehills.

BINDING ADJUSTMENT

The binding must grip the boot firmly to keep it from slipping forward, particularly when descending. If the boot slides forward, the heel strap can drop off the heel and let the boot slip backward out of the binding on the next step, or the boot toe will ride up on the toe bar, depressing the toe of the snowshoe and causing it to

Figure 8.
Binding should hinge freely up and down,
with toe of boot fitting through toe hole in
snowshoe and ball of foot directly over the
toe cord/pivot.

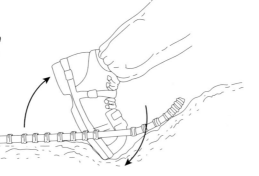

catch. No matter what kind of bindings you have, you need to know the basics of how to adjust them.

Because of the number of different bindings used on the many modern Western snowshoes marketed today, it is wise to first check the manufacturer instructions and/or have the shop personnel explain the proper way to attach the binding to your boot. There are too many combinations of straps, loops, buckles, ratchets, and laces to describe all the possibilities.

Developing expertise at tightening the bindings while standing on the snowshoe is a must. Wiggle the binding side to side after strapping the snowshoe to your boot to check for slack. This is the best time—before you are on the trail—to do the adjusting.

No matter how firmly the binding is buckled to the boot, it will not work properly if there is slack in the attachment of the binding to the snowshoe, especially on wood-frame designs. The binding must be kept tight on the toe cord or binding hinge. Straps wear and stretch, periodically developing slack. Before you strap on the boots, work the slack out of the straps that hold the binding to the toe cord. On some models thongs must be tightened; on others the slack in the heel strap is pulled through the leather of the binding.

After you have walked the first couple hundred yards of the day, double-check your binding adjustment. With experience, you will be able to feel whether the snowshoes are adjusted correctly. Just before starting a long descent, check for slack and tighten the bindings so you won't slide forward and slip out of a heel strap.

TYPES OF BINDINGS

Figure 9 is an improved **H binding,** one of the most popular bindings for wood-frame snowshoes. The boot is held firmly, but it can come out of the binding if you fall forward. The boot toe can slip back from under the toe strap, or on a steep sidehill the boot heel may rotate sideways, allowing the boot to slip from under the toe strap.

It takes some doing to put these bindings on your snowshoes the first time, so make sure they come with an instructional diagram if you buy them separately from the snowshoes. Once the binding is

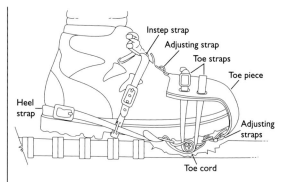

Figure 9. Improved H binding

on the snowshoe, slip your boot into it, with straps unbuckled, so that the ball of the foot is just behind or on the snowshoe toe cord. Center your boot in the toe hole so that it doesn't touch lacing on either side. Lift the heel and make sure the boot toe doesn't touch the toe bar. Tighten the toe strap firmly on the boot toe, then the heel strap, and last the instep strap. All buckles should be on the outside of your boot so strap ends won't catch on the other snowshoe and trip you. Recheck the

BIGfoot Says ▶▶

It will be much easier to understand how to adjust the bindings on new or rental snowshoes if you do it first in the comfort of your own home. Practice with the boots you will be wearing to avoid surprises that could arise in below-freezing or blizzard conditions.

bindings soon after you start your hike. If your boot toe catches on the toe bar when going downhill, loosen the heel strap, slide the boot back, and tighten the toe strap, then retighten other straps.

To remove your snowshoes, unbuckle the heel and instep straps and slide your boot out. If you will be using the same boot each time you snowshoe, you can leave the toe strap adjustment as is. When set up this way, the H binding is the fastest to put on and take off. If the straps are long enough, you can also make any adjustments without removing your mittens.

Several bindings similar to the improved H are available. However, one such binding, the **standard H,** does not have the toe piece that traps the boot toe and prevents it from sliding forward to catch on the toe bar. This toe piece is probably most useful on soft-toe shoe pacs rather than hard-toe climbing boots because it is painful to tighten the toe strap down really tight on your toes when wearing soft footgear. On level or gentle terrain there is little likelihood that the boot will slide forward out of the binding anyway; this is chiefly a problem when descending steep mountain slopes.

There is a limit to how tight the toe strap may be tightened. It must slide around the toe cord to allow the hinging action. If it is so tight that the tail of the snowshoe rises off the snow with each step, loosen the toe strap or check the instruction sheet to be sure the binding is mounted correctly.

The **wet noodle binding** (Figure 10) is, like the H binding, an old standby that is

Figure 10. Wet noodle binding

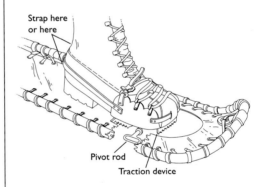

Figure 11. Western binding with extension attached to snowshoe

available at most shops all across the Snow Belt. Most people adjust it the same way as the H, tying the lace in one place and unbuckling the heel strap to remove the snowshoe. There is not a good way to keep the boot from sliding forward on steep descents, however, so this binding is better used on gentle terrain.

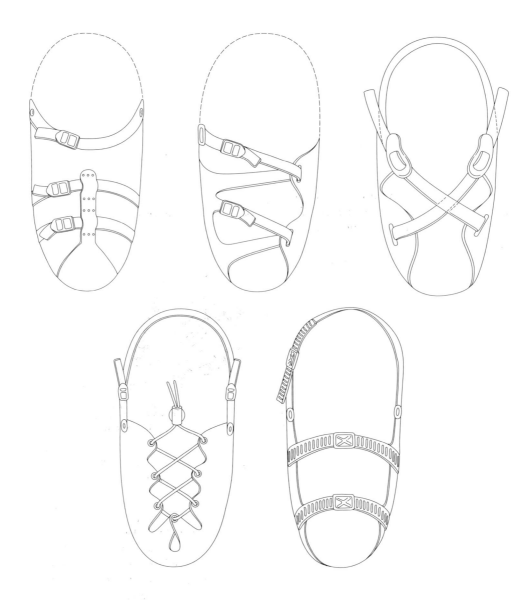

Figure 12. A small sample of various combinations and mixtures of bindings and heel strap possibilities on modern Western snowshoes. Mix and match!

The **Western binding** design in Figure 11 has been proven in the field since the 1950s and is an improvement on previous binding designs. Western snowshoes come equipped with that original binding shown or with the many other possible designs and combinations shown in Figure 12. A few Western bindings are available for use on wood snowshoes, with factory modifications for attachment to the toe cord. Just be sure all are compatible before purchasing.

The improved original Western binding (Figure 11) is actually updated from the wet noodle binding (Figure 10). The toe portion was enlarged, stronger materials used, the holes replaced with hooks and D-rings, and the thong changed to a strap and buckle. This binding fits well with most boot sizes and types.

The most secure method of tightening this Western binding onto your boot is as follows: Place the boot in the binding with the boot toe protruding through the binding about 1 inch. Then tighten the heel strap so the boot can't slip backward. Place the heel strap in the groove between sole and upper; if there is no groove, move the strap up to the Achilles tendon area, 2 to 3 inches above the boot heel (Figure 11).

Now tighten the toe strap through the hooks or D-rings, at the same time pulling the boot firmly back against the heel strap. To tighten the adjustment, raise your boot heel and wiggle it against the heel strap while pulling with both hands on the generous toe strap. Keep the boot heel centered on the snowshoe. This binding has buckles with spring-loaded latches, which automatically grip the strap and hold the adjustment.

These basic instructions apply to most new Western binding systems, the differences being attributed to types of laces, buckles, and loops, and which end you start tightening the binding. Again, be sure you follow the manufacturer's recommendations so your heel and toe straps don't loosen and fall off en route.

All this binding to the boot is then attached to the snowshoe at the toe cord by what is called a **binding hinge system.** Western snowshoes use two basic systems, with a few modifications. One is called a pivoting or rotating toe cord, the other a fixed toe cord. Modifications may include dual capabilities, spring-loaded double toe cords, and some adjustable devices.

The **pivoting** or **rotating toe cord** actually resembles the hinging action of the long wood-frame snowshoes. Because of the more stable Western binding, dropping or dragging of the tail on snow is not needed for directional purposes, but does allow snow to slide off the tail and the front tip to rise up over the next step of

BIGfoot Says ▶▶

To allow your foot to move naturally when you walk on snowshoes, place the ball of your foot directly over the toe cord/hinge. If the ball of the foot is too far back, it creates a toe grabbing effect, which causes a shuffling stride that can tire your arch and Achilles tendon and cause soreness.

snow. This is an advantage in deep powdery snow and in the backcountry. For running, however, the pivoting action can cause the snowshoe tip to hit the shins during a running stride.

The **fixed-hinge toe cord** does not allow the tail to drag on the snow as the foot is lifted for the next step, nor does it cause the shin-pounding action when running. Larger model snowshoes with a fixed toe cord may allow some snow to slide off the tail once they are broken in or if they are less taut. Otherwise, this fixed hinge will tend to snap back with each aggressive step, flipping snow onto your backside. In deep snow, you have to lift the foot higher to get the tip over the snow on the next step. This binding hinge is therefore best suited for packed trails and is great for jogging or running.

Some modifications of the hinge are designed to eliminate the undesirable snow flipping, snowshoe dragging (a minor problem on a slick surface), and shin bruising. One system cannot solve all problems, so pick what will be the best for your use.

Snowshoers frequently set their boots as far forward in the bindings as they can without catching their boot toes on the front decking or crosspiece. This is so they can stick their boot toe as far down as possible into the snow when they take a step, increasing their traction in steep places. This can be an advantage in climbing, but the benefit is offset somewhat because the boot slides forward when descending, increasing the chance of walking out of the

Figure 13. Old Canadian racing snowshoes with lampwick binding, which can also be used as an emergency binding

bindings. No firm rule of thumb need be dreamed up here. Snowshoe performance is increased by making small compromises. Those who put their boot toes as far forward in their bindings as possible probably have the point of view that if you can't get up the slope, your snowshoes won't fall off your boots coming back down it! With experience and some careful study, you will become more proficient at putting your snowshoes on in the morning so that they will need no additional tightening or adjusting until you take them off in the evening.

Few wood snowshoes are sold equipped with bindings, in contrast to Western snowshoes. Most wood snowshoes have a standard toe-hole dimension and accept several binding designs. Some Canadian snowshoes, particularly racing models for example, do not have the rectangular toe hole and are designed for the lampwick binding (Figure 13).

The **lampwick** and **squaw hitch bindings** are virtually unknown outside eastern Canada and New England, where the lampwick is used for "traditional" snowshoe races. It can be a good emergency binding, and when properly tightened to the boot it will hold well and hinge excellently. It is used in races from sixty yards to ten miles, including hurdles.

Most snowshoers can overlook much of what I've written about bindings designed for rugged snowshoeing. Plenty of people enjoy a level hike and aren't going to travel very many miles. It's possible to get inexpensive, lightweight snowshoes with simple bindings and lightweight shoe pacs and be quite a few dollars—not to mention pounds on the foot—ahead.

When you're not planning to traverse mountain country with a bunch of tigers trying to bag a couple of peaks before the next storm strikes, you don't have to have all that fancy gear. You will have time to stop and tighten a binding, put a patch on a blister, and share the beauty of the place with your companions.

But if you do plan to tackle tough country, the best is none too good. If you're in top shape, moving in a fast party, have really great conditions, and are heading to a special viewpoint about half an hour ahead, you'll be distressed if you flounder and fall due to a loose or poorly fitted binding. It's fatiguing to be fussing with your gear while being passed by a first-time snowshoer walking effortlessly because he or she has first-rate equipment and every thing is working just right.

The purpose of being out in the backcountry is to see, smell, and experience the beauty of winter, not to study the deficiencies of some old ragtag snowshoe bindings.

> **BIGfoot Says** ▸▸
>
> Remember that in the backcountry you must be prepared. There is no AAA or 911 quick response. Your cell phone will probably be out of range unless you are on satellite, and the GPS batteries may have died. You have to be able to get out on your own and without endangering others.

CHAPTER 4

Tubbs Snowshoe Company

Aids for Traction, Balance, and Power

A real landmark for the two of us who purchased Yukons in December 1950 was a four-day trip up Ingalls Creek to Mount Stuart, the 9,415-foot peak dominating central Washington's Cascade mountains. Conditions for snowshoeing were good, with the exception of icy depressions under each tree where the drip of snow melting off the branches had refrozen. Our new "guaranteed-not-to-sag" snowshoes didn't bite into the ice at all, and we slipped considerably. But quick sprints created enough momentum to effectively cross these minor difficulties. Early in the trip, however, it was obvious that one section of hard snow would be sufficient to seriously hamper progress up the trail.

Also in the area was a trapper whose boot imprint, with crisscross webbing

◀◀ ▲ *Using poles adds traction, balance, and power.*

under it, showed clearly in each snowshoe track. Apparently his rawhide webbing sagged badly but provided excellent, if temporary, traction. This certainly wasn't a satisfactory solution, because sagging rawhide soon breaks, but it did indicate that a small area that could bite into hard snow prevented the sliding we were experiencing.

Other snowshoers and I began a lengthy trial-and-error process of bolting, lacing, and tying different types of rough and sharp-edged objects so they would protrude below the bottom of the wood snowshoe and bite into hard snow (Figure 14). We tried attaching small pieces of aluminum angles to the frames at different curves and angles, wrapping rope and rawhide around the frames, and adding knotted rope to the webbing under the boot. Although these modifications helped, they were not enough.

60

The aluminum angles worked effectively except for one problem: walking is more comfortable and efficient if the foot, especially the ball of the foot, can be placed directly on top of any slightly higher point in a trail for the greatest traction. A traction angle attached to the toe bar is about 6 inches in front of the ball of the foot and must be placed where it will get the best grip. In places with tricky footing—crossing a stream on icy stepping stones or a slippery foot log—it was obvious that the traction should be directly under the foot so that the entire body weight would force the device to bite into the ice or hard crust. Not only did this new traction positioning prove more comfortable and efficient, but also it was possible to use a smaller and lighter device than one placed on the toe bar or frame. The traction must be effective in all directions so it will hold when going straight up or down, traversing, or angling

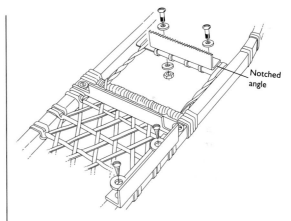

Notched angle

Figure 14. Traditional home workshop traction devices installed on bottom of frame and toe bar. Not all of these pieces are necessary at once.

uphill. A single smooth, straight bar is useless when sidehilling; on a hard crust it will act like a sled runner, speeding you on your way.

61

Snowshoers in the East also arrived at a solution to the traction problem. The toughest conditions for snowshoeing are normal in eastern mountain areas. By New Year's, cold temperatures create acres of ice on rock slabs, and each seep of water in a trail freezes into yards of ice. Trails in this area don't conform to the switchback ethic, and there are miles of trail that go straight up steep hills with a thicket of stunted trees on either side—known as Krummholz—that can't be penetrated on snowshoes. The ground above tree line is often not as steep, and summits and ridges are rounded, but generally the area is sheathed in rime ice, an ice crust that forms when clouds cover the area above tree line in subfreezing weather. The January thaw warms things briefly before temperatures plunge to subzero again, encrusting snow from valley floor to tree line.

An instep crampon lashed to the snowshoe webbing directly under the binding is required equipment under these eastern conditions. No serrated or smooth angle aluminum is sufficient to dent the case-hardened crust on these low-elevation, but quite formidable, mountains. The 5- or 6-inch-long steel points on the crampon are superb for the trail problems of ice and crust and the equal of most other traction devices in soft snow. However, above tree line and on slides, boot crampons normally replace snowshoes.

These instep crampons can be hard to find, but are not hard to install once found. Check with your local mountaineering shop or snowshoe dealer for climbing or

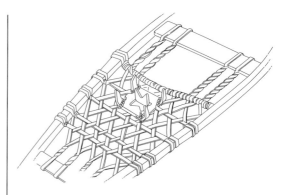

Figure 15. Crampon lashed to laced snowshoe

metal-frame snowshoe cleat parts. Figure 15 shows a simple way to lash crampons to the snowshoe webbing. Most of these crampons are tempered carbon steel, so it is not possible to bore holes in them.

One of the early popular Western snowshoes had a shallow, serrated, three-sided traction device or claw, or a spike crampon arrangement factory-made as an integral part of the metal hinge (Figure 16, lower snowshoe). This was a satisfactory unit, and, combined with the Western binding, it provides excellent control of the snowshoe. For soft snow and moderate crust this product was quite adequate—I'd have given an arm for it back in 1950 when I was sliding and crashing in icy tree holes on my first memorable outing.

A few Western snowshoes have a serrated angle the width of the snowshoe. This serves as the front crosspiece, or is attached to the crosspiece, putting it directly under the ball of the foot, where it

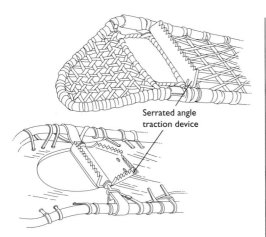

Serrated angle
traction device

*Figure 16. Earlier Western snowshoes with
serrated angle traction devices attached*

is nearly as effective as the three-sided traction described above, but it does not provide lateral grip.

The traction devices for the modern metal-framed snowshoes are evolving into many combinations and shapes of claws, cleats, and spikes (Figure 17). Most are trying to address the need for traction to grab on the ascents, brake on the descents, and provide lateral stability on the traverse.

The devices are usually made out of either lightweight aluminum or stronger hardened steel. A few are made of titanium, which is light and tough but expensive. Traction has been built into some decking materials that have a ribbed effect. Molded plastic snowshoes include significant traction in the mold design so there is less to add on during manufacturing.

During some snow conditions, even the best snow-repelling designs can't keep a metal claw from icing up. As snow and ice accumulate, your height increases while balance and traction deteriorate. This accumulation needs to be knocked off often or it just gets worse. To help shed the ice and snow on those wet, icy days, spray the metal claws and cleats with an all-natural, nonstick cooking spray before you start out on the trail.

It is obvious that traction devices are among the greatest aids to snowshoeing on varied terrain. The unmodified wood-frame snowshoe or a lightly cramponed metal-frame type performs comfortably on a very low slope, and there seems to be a steep or icy spot on every trip, regardless of how short or easy it is supposed to be. If you are tensed up, edging the snowshoes, and bent forward from the waist with hands extended to catch yourself when—not if—you slip, you will soon be too tired to proceed. The energy drain from tension is tremendous. It is acceptable to be tired after covering a lot of miles, but not to become totally

BIGfoot Says ▶▶
When the temperature is just at freezing or warmer, spray the metal claws with nonstick cooking spray or rub on white petroleum jelly before putting your snowshoes on the snow. It won't totally prevent icing up, but will make it easier to knock off ice and snow. A caution when snowshoeing with your furry friends: dogs love to lick off these coatings.

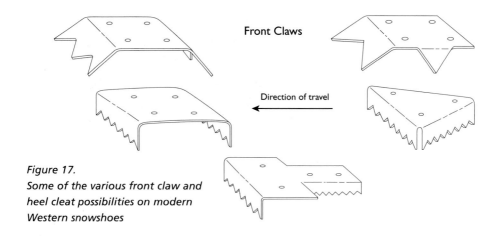

Front Claws

Direction of travel

Figure 17.
Some of the various front claw and
heel cleat possibilities on modern
Western snowshoes

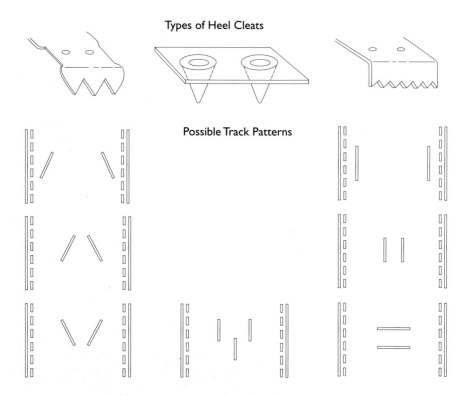

Types of Heel Cleats

Possible Track Patterns

exhausted on a short, steep pitch because of insufficient traction. It is also not acceptable to slow down a group continually while you are helped over hard parts, although it is proper and virtuous of the strong and well-equipped not to walk off and leave the weak and inexperienced party member floundering on an icy patch like a bug sprayed with insecticide. All this fatigue can be avoided with good traction from a positive and secure traction device, which makes it possible to snowshoe on slopes as steep as the ones you hike in summer.

A point to remember when choosing modern Western snowshoes with all the various choices of traction devices already attached is that the lower the skill, the greater the need for extra traction. With experience you can foresee rough spots and place the snowshoes in such a way that they will hold; an expert in good physical condition can do amazing things with poor equipment. On the other hand, a beginner on the best of modern snowshoes and traction devices can make the old-timer with rope wrapped around his frames look very old indeed.

POLES AND AXES

Another piece of equipment vital to maintaining balance in precarious positions is either a pair of ski-type poles or an ice ax with a ski pole basket attached (Figures 18 and 19). The expert snowshoer can stand on one snowshoe on a steep slope and gracefully swing the other web around

BIGfoot Says ▶▶
There is no reason to be in two-wheel drive while in four-wheel-drive country. In mountainous terrain or deep snow, using one pole or an ice ax will provide you a power assist only. Using double poles, however, will give you fully available balance and power, making snowshoeing much easier.

for a kick turn, but this may be impossible for a beginner. For both beginner and expert, the stability gained by using ski-type poles or an ice ax with basket means easier traveling on difficult terrain and less fatigue to endure.

The use of two, or double, poles won't seem natural or comfortable at first for some folks. After all, through evolution we have learned to walk upright—without our knuckles dragging on the ground—and if we have poles in our hands, how can we be free to swing on the branches overhanging the snowshoe trail? However, with practice, double poles become an extension of our arms, making travel much easier out on the mountain trails and deep snow, and giving us greater balance and more power to the legs. (See more on technique in Chapter 8.)

Whether ascending or descending, double poles can give you an extra boost while also being a safety aid. If you fall down in deep snow, it can be very difficult to get up, especially if you are in an odd position. Don't try to plant your poles upright with your arms way up in the air

Make an X with your poles to aid getting up after a fall in deep snow.

and struggle to pull yourself up. You could possibly bend or break your poles, and just how many pull-ups a day do you do to really have enough strength? Use the following method for more efficiency: First, relax and catch your breath. Second, take off your pole straps. Third, get your snowshoes on the downhill side of your body. Fourth, make an "X" with your poles as shown above. This is like having a giant basket on the end of your arm instead of shoving your arm deep into the snow up to your shoulder.

The two groups that find poles not to their advantage are runners and young children. As long as a racecourse is mostly over packed snow, runners prefer the freedom of arm movement. Kids are built low to the ground and don't have as much upper body strength, so poles just get in the way.

Heavy-duty backcountry poles, adjustable in length (see photo at right) and with large baskets, are the type to buy.

Poles with adjustable length make a long traverse on a steep hill much easier.

Downhill poles are better than nothing, but the small baskets sink much deeper than larger ones and some do not have wrist straps. Using the wrist straps as you would for cross-country skiing gives you power on uphills and downhills without having to grip the poles so tight. The grip can be loose and the hands relaxed.

For those doing a lot of backcountry snowshoeing in avalanche-prone areas, consider the poles that have removable baskets and can be screwed together to form avalanche probes.

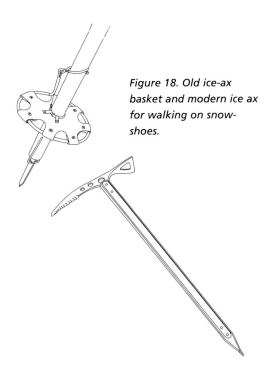

Figure 18. Old ice-ax basket and modern ice ax for walking on snow-shoes.

elastic cord that hooks onto the glide ring stop and requires no tools at all. Be sure that the center hole in the basket is large enough to permit your ax shaft to slide through it—some are too small.

During very cold weather, a metal ice ax head tends to chill the hand. A solution is to cement eighth-inch, closed-cell foam on the head. Leaving the tip of the pick and adze uncovered makes the covering less likely to peel off when the ax is used to chop steps or level a tent platform. A good set of poles may be much easier to find and use than an ice ax, in addition to providing more useful balance and power.

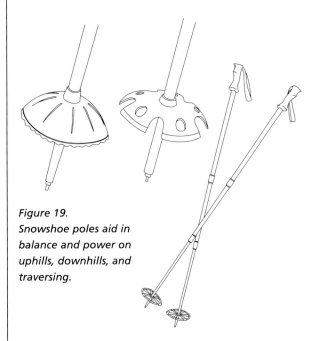

Figure 19. Snowshoe poles aid in balance and power on uphills, downhills, and traversing.

A number of mountain climbers who snowshoe also use ice axes. But, this tool is of no use in deep, soft snow unless it is long enough to use as walking support and has a large basket attached, thus making it a practical part of a snowshoer's equipment. Ice-ax baskets are now very hard to find and you may have to make it yourself or describe how it should be constructed. It should be designed to be attached to the ice ax without drilling holes, which weaken the shaft. One attachment method is to use a radiator hose–style clamp to tighten the basket to the shaft, requiring a screwdriver for installation or removal. Another has an

CHAPTER 5

Carl Heilman II / Wild Visions, Inc.

Clothing

Mountains have great variation of slope and snow conditions, and just as the snowshoe best adapted to the widest range of conditions is the one to get, so must clothing be chosen. Mountain weather seems to change from one extreme to another. Each area of the Snow Belt has a winter weather pattern considered "normal" by the natives. My observation of normal winter weather is that this pattern probably holds true 51 percent of the time, which leaves up to 49 percent that is not normal.

As an example, I was rained on in New Hampshire, British Columbia, and Washington in January and February of 1979. This is not normal in two of these locations. So the solution seems to be this: prepare for subzero weather but don't be

◀◀ ▲ *On Algonquin Peak in the Adirondack High Peak Region with Mount Marcy in the background*

surprised if a heat wave strikes, the temperature vaults to above freezing, and it rains. Keep things as simple as possible by using garments that are both most adaptable to extreme cold and water-repellent.

In the East, "normal" winter temperatures are about 0° F, with –5° to –10° at tree line and 20- to 30-mph wind on ridges and summits. The Canadian Rockies and interior British Columbia are about the same, but with less wind except on summits. The Rockies and associated ranges of the United States are similar, with warmer daytime temperatures toward the south. The Sierra probably won't have extreme cold as often as the ranges farther north. The wet, snowy Cascades generally are the warmest winter range.

Residents of western Wyoming, where the temperature has reached –60° F, believe they have the coldest minimum temperature. Minnesota, Wisconsin, and Michigan (especially the Upper Peninsula) have recorded minimums near −50° F—not as cold, but the locals feel the consistency of subfreezing temperatures in the region is noteworthy. Actually, conditions vary so much in winter that if you wait a few days or weeks, the type of weather you're looking for will probably come. Alaska and the Canadian Yukon require expeditions and are somewhat beyond the limits of snowshoeing as described in this book.

Generalizations are hard to make, but as temperatures dip below 0° F, you are permitted fewer mistakes outdoors. Somewhere around −30° F in still air, any mistakes will probably result in frostbite or worse. With wind, similar damage occurs at higher temperatures because of the chill factor: in a stiff wind, the thermometer may read 10° F or 15° F, but the effective temperature is −30° F.

Severity and duration of storms is probably more significant than minimum temperatures and maximum snowfall. Remember that the farther north you go, the shorter the winter days, generally the lower the temperature extreme, and the greater the length of storm. Snowshoers taking just day trips will likely remain in valleys and on lower summits, so they have less concern about clothing and weather than those snowshoers who take longer treks or climb higher summits.

A system of clothing should be devised that is adaptable to extremes of temperature, yet light in weight and requiring only minutes to adjust. The exertion of climbing or breaking trail through deep, loose snow generates sweat. Moisture, from sweat or melting snow, is the greatest problem connected with keeping warm in winter.

FABRICS

Wool, an old-time favorite of many, is no longer in complete possession of first choice for pants, shirts, sweaters, mitts, socks, and caps. The many wool devotees will probably ensure its position at the top of the list for some things, but it now must share a place with synthetic garments. Wool is a desirable fabric for outdoor clothing because it contains a springy fiber that retains trapped air, which gives it a broad temperature comfort range and the ability to insulate well even when wet. However, wool also has a saturation point, when the fiber will not hold any more moisture, and it gets very heavy when wet and takes an extra long time to dry out. Wool layers well with polyester fleece over it.

While some synthetics may work best for outer garments, a few people still enjoy the feel of all wool or wool blends for long-johns, and the best socks for winter are made of mostly wool. For socks, that springy wool fiber provides the best warmth and wicking on a sweaty foot. A poly-type wicking liner can be used if itchiness is a problem.

BIGfoot Says ▶▶
The new uses of wool highlight the special softness of merino wool (from a type of long-haired sheep) in garments and socks that can be run through a washer and dryer, and wools laminated to outer garment fabrics.

BIGfoot Says ▶▶
Many synthetics have very fancy trade names for magical combinations, special processes, durable coatings, and high-tech laminations. Always refer to their fabric content, type of weave, and claims for reaction to the elements before making buying decisions.

Polyester fleece or **pile** provides comparable insulation, can be woven into any thickness, and has several advantages. It is not itchy or allergenic; it is much lighter in weight and more elastic, adding to the wearer's comfort; it dries quickly; and it wicks sweat away from your body better than wool. Polyester fleece that is wet from extreme sweating, from rain, or from melting snow can actually be shaken almost dry since the fiber cannot hold moisture at all. Once major moisture is shaken off, body heat can further the drying process. The fleecing of the fabric actually adds airspace, or fluff, for insulation, like the furry and feathered creatures do naturally in the winter.

Polypropylene garments were originally designed for use as long-underwear tops and bottoms. This is another fiber that will not hold moisture; therefore, with the warmth of the body, moisture is transferred from the skin out to the air or the next layer of clothing. Polypro is so comfortable that it has been worn in layers and also as the outer shirt and pants for a number of snowshoers. Some people wear them tight, some wear them loose.

However worn, polypropylene garments can serve as the foundation for a system of clothing that is quickly adjustable to temperature changes.

One drawback of polypro material in older garments is its ability to retain and intensify body odors. When switching from wool to polypropylene, you exchange a wet-dog odor for the smell of ancient unwashed socks or a locker room. The newer models, improved to almost elimi-nate the odor problem, should be washed as often as possible. Polypropylene is easier to wash and dries much faster than wool.

Coated or treated **polyester** has replaced polypro as the preferred fabric by some undergarment manufacturers. They have no odor problems and are more easily machine washed and dried. Polyester has also been combined and/or laminated with other fabrics, primarily nylon, to "push-pull" moisture away from the skin.

A word of caution about **cotton** in the winter: although it has been many snowshoers' favorite fabric to wear next to the skin—as a turtleneck, T-shirt, or socks—it is not a wicking fabric. Moisture just remains in the fabric next to the skin and gets cold and can even freeze. In socks,

cotton flattens, becomes abrasive, and conducts cold quickly. Thick cotton can feel warm as a layer, but is never useful in the winter when wet, especially if one is close to hypothermia. Leave cotton for the summer heat.

Since none of the above fabrics are really windproof or water-repellent, the discussion turns now to **nylon** and outer garments. The nylon-cotton materials of the past have given way to tightly woven nylons, treated or coated nylons, and nylons laminated with various waterproof, breathable plastics. The ultimate laminates allow moisture vapor from your body to vent through microsopic holes while preventing larger raindrops or snowmelt from penetrating. Keep in mind, though, that we are the only animal that puts on a plastic bag when the weather gets bad. Also, breathability is only relative to being waterproof. In many cases protection from the wind is of the utmost importance if you are insulated well enough.

Another fabric used for outer garments is a group called **microfibers,** which are mostly of polyester, with some of nylon. Microfiber fabric is woven so tightly that it repels wind and water while retaining breathability without coatings or laminates. As a shell, these garments are extremely light weight.

A word of caution about buying water-proof, coated outer garments. Moisture from your body can condense inside the garment, usually as frost in winter, and leave you as wet on a cold, dry day as if you were being rained on in a leaky jacket.

BIGfoot Says ▶▶

For winter activity, cotton has been referred to as "the death cloth"! When wet it does not insulate, it does not dry easily in the cold, and it can freeze while you are wearing it. Save it for summer.

Vent often and learn to slow your pace to regulate body temperature and oversweating.

LAYERING

The importance of layering comes down to two main points. First, clothing layers can be put on or taken off to adjust for changing weather conditions. Second, in addition to the layers themselves, it is the air space in between that adds insulation. Snowshoeing is a very warm activity while you are moving, yet you can get chilled very fast when you stop. Remove layers before you get too hot and put them back on before you get cold.

For anything less than expeditions and extreme cold conditions, apply this simple rule of layering: two layers on the bottom with three layers on top. Long underwear counts as one layer; however, rain or wind gear should be considered extra. When you know it is going to be extra cold, use thicker layers or use an additional thin layer.

Just as we have to start at the base of any mountain to reach the top, we can approach clothing layers from the same direction—from the bottom up. We have discussed fabrics and their advantages; now we can layer them for comfort and safety during conditions most encountered across the Snow Belt of the northern United States and lower Canada. If you are planning a snowshoe trek of expedition proportions in extreme terrain, conditions, and cold, you will need more advice from other sources. You should then check with your local mountain shops and guide services for the best recommendations.

The correct **socks** become the best foundation for a comfortable day. Your feet will need to be warm and dry. Under most conditions, two layers of socks will be enough. Next to the foot, a thin wicking layer of light wool or a poly fabric will transfer moisture to the thicker insulating outer sock. The most popular insulating socks are either a rag-wool blend or merino wool, both of which are very soft and comfy. Some people may prefer an acrylic blend, but never use cotton. Polyester fleece is also being used, as are neoprene-type booties. To compensate for colder temperatures, some people tend to add thicker or more socks to a boot they have fitted for warmer times. This is a bad idea because it can make the boot too tight, cutting off circulation in the feet and making them colder. Make sure both socks and boots are compatible and provide proper foot room. Take extra socks in case your feet get wet, especially on overnights and long trips.

Next, we have two layers of **pants,** with the first being long johns next to the skin to wick out to the next layer. Refer to the fabric section above for more information on the materials available for this base layer. For the second layer, there can be many choices depending on conditions, activities, and preferences. Loose-fitting knickers or long pants of almost any fabric but cotton can be used, from wool to polyester blends, laminates, and fleeces.

Snowshoeing is a wet activity when the snow is deep in the backcountry or you are running down a packed trail. Snow will fly up and stick to fleecy or shaggy materials, making for very wet bottoms. A hard-finish wool pant repels snow somewhat better, but a slicker surface is probably more desirable to shed the snow. A nylon outer shell is the best for those conditions. For running it may be comfortable to have the shell as the second layer. For most other purposes the shell becomes the third layer. Shells should have full-length zippers so they can be taken off with boots and snowshoes still on or quickly removed when entering a tent or building. As the conditions get colder, it might be necessary to add more insulating layers. Make sure your clothing does not become too tight, which takes away that insulating layer of air or just makes it difficult to move freely.

The **upper body** frequently needs the most adjustment throughout the day and is where layering becomes most critical to protect the vital organs and regulate body heat and cooling. To keep the upper body warm, again start with a **wicking** or **moisture-transferring undergarment** that will keep your skin dry. Choose the type of neck opening to match the conditions or your metabolism. A crewneck works well for overheaters and warm spring days; turtlenecks keep warmth in and snow out; and zippered turtlenecks are the most versatile.

There are varying fabric thicknesses to choose from on the market. If you have two, make one thin and the other thicker in order to layer. The second layer will be for **insulation and trapping air** between it and the first layer. A polyester fleece or pile is the best choice for lightness, continuing the transfer of moisture to the outside air for evaporation and quick drying. Wool shirts have been a tradition in some areas, but they do not dry very well if wet from sweat or the elements, so keep wool as dry as possible. Again, do not use cotton in the winter. When wet, it will not insulate, and it can freeze!

The choices for the third and possibly a fourth layer are numerous. If you wear two layers of undergarments, a fleece or pile garment might be the third. Another **fleece** or **pile** could be substituted for the second undergarment. Keep in mind that the secret here is to layer lightweight, moisture-transferring, insulating fabrics that will trap layers of air.

Under some conditions, the top layer may need to block the wind and/or keep out wet snow or rain. This is where the outer shell comes out of your pack. As discussed in the fabric section above, this can include nylons and polyesters that are untreated, coated, laminated, with layers, or as microfibers. Your choices here may have to be based on expected conditions, preference, and pocketbook—with assistance from your local mountain shop.

Down jackets or parkas have been an old favorite to put on when stopping for a break on the trail in cold weather, or as the ultimate protection above tree line in subzero temperatures and wind. Down is first choice in cold dry climates, but if it gets wet, the down mats and, like cotton, loses its insulating quality. Keep it in a waterproof stuff sack in your pack, and put a water-repellent shell over it if there is a chance it will get wet.

In wet-winter areas, polyester batting, which has springy fibers like wool, is a better choice in a jacket or parka than down. It is available in various thicknesses. Several types of quilted insulating material marketed under different trade names are available, varying in price and amount of warmth.

For the hands, polyester fleece with wool mitts and shell outers are a versatile combination. Inners made of these fabrics combined with separate gauntlets are close to the equal of the down mitts, which are traditionally regarded as the ultimate in warmth. The inners also can be dried more easily than down mitts.

Outer mitts, whether shell or insulated, should have heavier waterproof, coated fabric at least on the palms and front of fingers and thumbs, if not the whole mitt. Wear on this part of the mitt can quickly shred lighter-weight fabric, laminates, or nylon.

Notice here that we are discussing mittens rather than gloves. In gloves, the fingers are on their own for insulation and warmth. In mittens, they keep each other warm by being naked and together. The thin polypropylene liner gloves are useful, however, for extra-sweaty hands and for protecting fingers from cold metal objects or when more manual dexterity is needed.

Never skimp on mitts and protection for your hands. Your hands are vital in the winter outdoors, and everything you touch seems to be either covered with snow or ice or is just cold.

It is important to have good headgear, since your body can lose as much heat from an uncovered head as your entire body produces at rest. A combination face mask and stocking cap, large enough to pull down over the ears or down to the neck, is a first choice when the weather is bad. Most face masks have eye holes, a

BIGfoot Says ▶▶

In most moderate weather conditions, rag-wool or poly fleece mitts are comfortable, but they can get damp from sweating or by touching and melting snow. So carry two pairs (a spare is always good for emergencies anyway). When one pair gets damp, put the mitts inside your shirt next to your chest and they will dry by the time your second pair gets wet.

Tubbs Snowshoe Company

Above tree line and at high altitude the sun is dangerously bright. Protect yourself with proper eyewear and clothing.

nose hole, and a mouth hole. Better is one with a wide opening that can expose the face from eyebrows to chin, or be closed to cover mouth and nose, with goggles to protect the eyes. The hood from your outer shell can give additional protection from the elements. A spare wool watch cap or polyester fleece cap can be used for less severe days. A billed cap with ear flaps is great protection from the sun.

Sunglasses or **goggles** are necessary to protect your eyes from direct sunlight and reflected glare, which can cause snow blindness. Side panels on sunglasses can be helpful not only for glare, but also for wind (see Chapter 12, on sunburn and windburn).

Goggles are not practical on New England ridge tops when rime ice is freezing out of the clouds, because it ices over the goggles, too. In very windy subzero temperatures, take care when exhaling—the wind can whip your moist breath around so that it freezes on your goggles and has to be scraped off. In high winds and below-zero temperatures, a neoprene or leather face mask may be desirable. People with tender skin can get nipped on the cheeks or nose at 0° F and 10- to 15-mph wind. Covering the nose and mouth with the mask, so that you breathe through a layer of wool, can help in severe cold and wind. It is a little sloppy when the wool gets soaked with moisture from your breath, but the exhaled air warms the wool, which in turn warms the next breath. Neoprene or leather face masks have small openings the breath goes through.

A homemade **snorkel** is useful in place of, or in addition to, the wool cap–face mask combination. This is a 6- or 8-inch length of wool sock, with the toe cut off and open, used as a breathing tube. Place one end over your mouth and nose and leave the other end dangling. The sock should be large enough to reach from just below your eyes to well below your chin, and held firmly in place with an elastic band stretched over your head. The snorkel is especially useful for sleeping. If your sleeping bag isn't quite warm enough, breathing cold air may be enough to cause you to spend a cold night.

It is important to discover how much clothing you need, as well as the temperature patterns of your area. By experimenting you can soon arrive at a combination that allows you to adapt to changing weather conditions without carrying too many pounds or spending too much money.

Gaiters are essential to cover the gap between pants cuff and boot top to keep snow out of your boots. There is less condensation under them if the upper part of the gaiter is of a breathable, snow-shedding fabric. The lower part should fit snugly against your boot and be made of a heavy-duty, waterproof material. Coated is fine. Some styles fit pacs well and others are better for mountaineering boots. Make sure they fit before you buy. (See gaiters in photo on page 82.)

Most gaiters have full-length zippers, perhaps covered by a flap that is held shut by snaps or Velcro™. Some have full-length Velcro without the extra flap or zipper. The easiest to put on have the closure on the front, where you can see it.

Some gaiters extend to the boot sole and have an elastic band sewn to the bottom, which holds it snug to the boot, and a strap under the instep to hold it down. These are warmer and more waterproof than the shorter gaiters.

Insulated or "super" gaiters are a must for extra-cold temperatures and travel on deep snow, especially at subzero temperatures. They increase the warmth of a single climbing boot to nearly the equal of the double mountaineering boot. Some super gaiters have a cable sewn into the bottom hem, which when tightened works into the groove between boot upper and sole, the "welt." Normally they are not as easy to put on as your regular gaiters, so they are left on for several trips. A front zipper provides access to the boot laces.

Super gaiters are essentially heavyweight nylon pack cloth overboots that extend up to the knee. Some are insulated and feature lug soles; others have neither. The insulated types are meant to be worn over light summer boots and may provide a practical solution for people who want winter-quality footwear without having to buy double mountaineering boots.

Long gaiters are necessary with knickers, because the long knicker socks, being of wool with a long nap, don't protect the lower leg from wind and become covered with snow, which melts. Knickers are comfortable, with little bind over the knee when you need to step very high, which is common in deep snow.

Keeping your feet warm isn't entirely up to the boots. If you have clothing that adequately warms your torso, legs, and arms, probably mediocre cold-weather footwear will be sufficient. If your blood is warm as it flows through your arms and legs, it will help keep your feet and hands warm. But the warmest boots and mitts won't keep feet and hands warm if you are standing around in wet cotton pants and a soaked shirt and jacket.

Of the several types of **footgear** used for snowshoeing, soft boots are probably the most popular for level terrain. The pac boot, with rubber lower and leather upper, was designed in New England and has long been a favorite for snowshoes. With plenty of wool socks and an insole, or with a felt liner, these boots are warm enough for the severest subzero as well as above-freezing temperatures. Pac boots and snowmobile boots that are constructed of rubber lowers and leather or fabric uppers don't really provide sufficient support for the foot and are quite heavy for long trips. When the bindings are tightened for mountain travel, the pressure is on the foot, rather than on the boot. Some people wouldn't use anything but pac boots, but for a person with really cold feet—like me—it takes a lot of socks, or a felt inner boot, to make them warm enough, and the binding will frequently bruise or blister the greatest pressure points (for blister treatment, see Chapter 12).

Newer versions of the pac boot are being called winter sports boots. They use synthetic rubber bottoms, heavy-duty nylon uppers with closed-cell foam insulation, and extra-thick polyester fleece liners. Some also use straps and buckles for fit adjustment. Like the pac boots, they are soft and warm, but a bit heavy.

Light- to medium-weight hiking boots, leather mountaineering boots, and some

---

BIGfoot Says ▶▶

Snowshoeing is basically a winter hike, so remember that any boot you use should be as comfortable on snowshoes as one you'd wear on a long hike.

insulated leather boots have become quite popular for snowshoeing. They are warm enough for winter use by people who don't have a cold-feet problem, and who use heavy-duty gaiters. Some of these boots have a waterproof, breathable liner while others might require a silicone spray or waxy paste-type coating for added protection.

The warmest boot currently available is probably the plastic double boot. Designed for mountaineering, the boot has a heavy lug sole and hard toe, so snowshoe or crampon bindings hold well and do not bruise the foot even when cinched down. These double boots are quite lightweight compared with the now nearly extinct leather model. The insulation is in the inner boot, similar to the felt liner in the pacs mentioned earlier. These liners fit quite well in the plastic outer, like pacs, and are probably warmer than the regular inner boot. The inner boots and socks will need to be dried each night since the plastic outer boot is impervious, as is the rubber or plastic bottom section of pacs.

Once the ultimate in cold-weather foot protection was the GI Korea boot, also called the Mickey Mouse, mouse, or bunny boot. It may still be available at some military surplus stores but is becoming scarce in some sizes. The boot was made with rubber or synthetic outer and inner layers with about three-eighths of an inch of insulation sealed between. As long as the insulation stayed dry, the boot was incredibly warm and rates first for protecting climbers' feet from frostbite on such peaks as Alaska's Mount McKinley.

The chief complaint about the mouse boot was the waterproof inner layer, which prevented evaporation of sweat so completely that your socks would probably be soaked by the end of the day, and wet equates with cold.

Be sure when camping out to use boots as a pillow or put them between sleeping bags or someplace else where they aren't chilled all night. Warming them in the sleeping bag before arising is unpleasant but often desirable. It's hard to get your feet warm after putting on boots with frost inside them from a frigid night.

On high peaks and in remote country, however, you are committed to several days, and you must have equipment for the storm that might catch you out there. By way of comparison, a lot of people who drown never expected be in water; some unexpected event placed them there. Those who survive such sudden events are usually prepared for them.

BIGfoot Says ▶▶

Easy hikes on warm, sunny days require much less clothing than snowshoeing on cold winter days. Nevertheless, your risk of hypothermia and discomfort from the cold isn't terribly great if you don't get too far from the road, allow plenty of time and energy to get back to your car, keep an eye on the weather, and don't go out when it is below zero in cold country (or below 25°F in warmer areas). The lack of proper clothing together with poor judgment equals unnecessary risk!

Tubbs Snowshoe Company

Layering makes it easier to modify your clothing needs to weather and temperature conditions.

Incidentally, improvisation is fine, but it can be carried to extremes. Avoid equipment or gimmicks cobbled on to something you already have that doesn't work right. These inventions give the appearance of increasing the adaptability of gear to many situations but often require constant adjusting and are too complicated to be practical. Try to pick out clothing that you adjust only when it becomes extremely cold, extremely windy, or extremely warm. Time spent fussing with gear is better saved for enjoying the scenery.

CHAPTER 6

Other Equipment

There are so many new models of tents, packs, sleeping bags, and stoves that it is difficult to keep up. The improvements have come so fast that many of us have outdated equipment that is only ten years old. Rather than list everything available, this text will cover some basics to look for. Consult equipment guides for detailed comparisons. Each writer has his or her favorites, which may not match your own.

TENTS

For general use in winter where high winds are no problem, there are so many tent designs that a choice appears difficult. However, it is of greatest importance to get the simplest pole assembly and the

◀◀ ▲ *Near Lake Colden in the Adirondacks high peak region*

most room for the least weight, without compromising safety for probable changing weather conditions. Snow travel is strenuous, and you will be carrying enough gear without adding unnecessary ounces to the load.

There are a lot of two-person, lightweight, and inexpensive two- or three-season tents on the market. But you should not expect a bargain-price tent to bear any snow load or wind! Generally, if you are planning to stay overnight on a snowshoe trip you should consider safety and comfort so you will have the ability and the desire to do it again. Check with your local mountain shops for recommendations covering the possible conditions in your area or destination. (See Figure 20, for tent shape possibilities on the market.)

High winds, found above tree line and particularly in New England and the Adirondacks, will flatten tents that aren't expedition quality, and some that are adequate for Alaska and the Himalaya. Heavy snowfall will have the same effect, unless you get out and shovel the snow off before damage is done.

Use the skills of the pioneers in winter camping to choose a spot in which to camp. Set your tent up where the natural features such as forest or rock outcrop will provide wind protection. This is a calculated risk above tree line since winds are notorious for not blowing the way you would expect them to. To be honest, there is very little in the way of wind protection above tree line; it seems to blow everywhere, first one direction and later another, until all points of the compass have been accounted for.

The majority of winter campers can pick forested places to camp that are protected from wind. Selecting such sites will ease the strain on your equipment budget.

If you do choose to buy an expedition-quality tent, keep in mind that not all expedition labels indicate better quality, so compare before buying. Real expedition tents have much reinforcing on seams and corners and may be of heavier fabric, so they will weigh and cost more. The heavier fabric also may be more windproof and water-repellent. Still, a lightweight tent can be protected during a heavy snowfall by shoveling or shaking the load off, and if you know the area and use the terrain to advantage, you won't need to lug a Himalaya-quality tent. Do remember, however, that sheltered places accumulate more snowfall than wind-blasted ridges and plateaus, so be prepared to dig out more often.

External frames, which are still one of the most useful modifications in tent design in the last thirty years, add more usable internal space. The advantage of

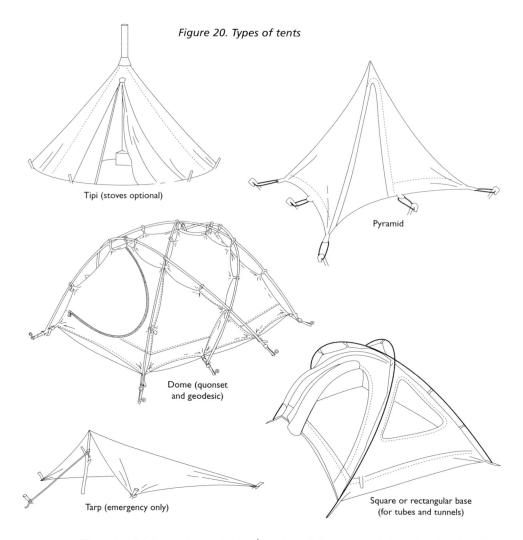

Figure 20. Types of tents

Tipi (stoves optional)

Pyramid

Dome (quonset
and geodesic)

Tarp (emergency only)

Square or rectangular base
(for tubes and tunnels)

more room offsets the debit of extra weight in poles. The frame makes it possible to hold the roof out so the lower third is like having an 18-inch vertical sidewall. This also eliminates the center pole and several outside guy ropes. All the sections of external frames are joined by slipping the small end of one into the large end of the next. Vital sections may get lost as the tent is collapsed and rolled up in the morning. The solution to this problem is to run a length of elastic shock cord through the hollow centers of each section, then attach it on the inside of each end section so that no piece can be misplaced (some models are made this way). If there is some tension on the shock cord it is easy to join the sections, especially when setting the tent up in a storm or after dark. If the tent has solid fiberglass pole sections, about all you can do is count carefully each time you take the tent down to be sure you have them all.

Quonset-like, dome-design, and tube or tunnel-type tents are now the most popular. They have a low profile, which makes some models extremely wind-resistant, and are surprisingly roomy inside for their small dimensions. Some very large and roomy geodesic-style tents seem ideal for winter camping in sheltered areas since the weight per person is less than when using two-person tents.

The average modern tent is made of nylon rather than cotton. Nylon can be lightweight, nearly windproof, quite water-repellent, and very strong. Coated fabrics have their problems: some are supposed to breathe but don't, and some coatings can peel.

Laminated fabrics have received wide acceptance. Sealing the seams and keeping the fabric clean seem to be the key to their qualities of being waterproof against rain yet permeable to vapor from body and breath, which keeps the inside of the tent amazingly dry. By avoiding the need for a rain fly, which is almost a necessity for other tents in winter, you save a couple of pounds of weight, but will add in total cost.

My present winter tent is a Quonset design made of laminated fabric. It does not leak in an all-night rainstorm, and with some ventilation, moisture and frost do not condense inside down to 0° F. Below zero, frost appears overnight. Under some conditions, ice can cover the outside and stop the tent from breathing. Its weight, 4 $\frac{1}{2}$ pounds, is good but headroom is poor. Putting on clothes in the morning is unpleasant with the frosty ceiling. However, no lightweight tent is going to be very roomy: for each plus factor of your equipment there is a compromise.

A rain fly is useful in near-melting or rainy winter weather, unless the tent is highly water-repellent. Essentially a tarp shaped to tie over the tent, this second layer of fabric sheds moisture and adds warmth. It also can be used as an extra ground cover inside the tent or to cover gear left outside. (It is desirable to stow all packs inside the tent to keep them from being buried in snow, although a small tarp can be used to cover these items outside.)

Use care to protect your tent's water-proof floor from cuts and scrapes, which will let moisture in. Foam pads provide floor insulation, making them far prefer-able to air mattresses and other unsuitable choices—such as boughs, which were vastly overrated even when considered environ-

BIGfoot Says ▶▶
A sponge is light to carry and handy to have for mopping the ceiling or floor of your tent in case of greenhouse effect.

mentally acceptable. An improvement is the self-inflating air/foam combination mattress, which is good down to –5° or –10° F. It is insulated as well as air-filled for comfort, and requires only a few puffs to fill (the old, noninsulated air mattresses were actually a way to sleep colder). In subzero cold a foam pad above or below your air/foam mattress will probably be a necessary addition.

Ventilation is required inside a tent. In a good tent that doesn't leak from the outside, it is frustrating to be wet simply because the occupants' breath and body heat generate enough moisture to condense on the walls —the so-called "greenhouse effect"—and drip on sleeping bags, occupants, and everything stored inside.

SLEEPING BAGS

Choosing a sleeping bag for winter depends mainly on how much warmth you need. You will probably have to guess what you'll need based on experience on previous summer camping trips. For some people a bag with two pounds of down or polyester batting is sufficient, but others require double that plus an insulated jacket as a blanket.

The insulating value of down or polyester depends on the amount of trapped air. Down is extremely lightweight, and when contained in a sleeping bag it has great insulating ability per pound of weight. Improved polyester-filled sleeping bags also deserve consideration. They are heavier than down bags of equal warmth, but they cost less. The main advantage of this synthetic fiber over down is its ability to insulate when wet.

When you are camping on snow for several nights, moisture will build up in the sleeping bag if there is no chance to dry your gear. Unlike synthetic fiber, a down bag will quickly mat and lose warmth. A sleeping bag cover of water-repellent laminate will help prevent moisture from condensing in the bag. Theoretically the moisture from your body will pass through the laminate and condense or freeze on the outside of the cover—but don't count on that happening consistently.

Sleeping bag manufacturers have written at great length on the relative warmth of different types of construction. All agree that when the two layers of cloth that contain the down or synthetic fiber are sewn through or quilted, the insulating value is reduced. Better is a system of inner and outer fabric separated by walls that, in effect, create separate tubes or boxes that allow the down or synthetic to fluff, or loft, with no sewn-through part where the filling is compressed. The warmest bags are those in which the individual separating walls of the tubes overlap. This construction prevents all but a few cold spots.

Simplicity, warmth, and roominess are of greatest importance in the sleeping bag. Frequently you will be chilled when you first get in the bag, so you may have removed only your jacket and wind parka. With insulated bodies crowded on either side, after a couple of hours you'll awaken, uncomfortably warm. If the bag is roomy enough, you can remove either your pants or shirt or both without unzipping the bag, and put them on again inside the bag the next day without exposing yourself to the cold morning air.

The penalty for warmth and comfort is usually weight and expense. It is pleasant to emerge fully dressed and warm from the insulated cocoon, hands warm and working efficiently to start the stove. The Spartan can survive in a tight, lightweight bag, especially for only one night, but winter nights are about twice as long as summer nights. It is not unusual to crawl into bed at 8:00 P.M. or earlier and remain there until it is light outside at 7:00 A.M. or later. If you are uncomfortable, these are long, dismal hours to suffer through.

Getting into your sleeping bag with wet or moist clothing is a mixed blessing. You will eventually become warmer and your clothes will get dryer, but the sleeping bag will get wetter. Thus the warmth of the final backup system—the sleeping bag—is sacrificed. It's better in the long run to carry extra clothing in waterproof bags and change into dry garments before crawling into the bag. It is also better to strip and get in the bag naked rather than get your sleeping bag wet unnecessarily. You'll warm up faster that way, too, since you won't be using body heat to dry out your clothes. The initial shock of cold fabric on bare torso is severe but fortunately brief.

The greatest problem in keeping a sleeping bag dry in winter, of course, is using it in subfreezing temperatures. Your body puts out moisture as vapor, even while sleeping. The vapor condenses in the sleeping bag and is more evident when the weather is cloudy and close to raining or snowing. At times of falling rain or snow, the problem is unspeakable. If the winter trip involves packing up camp and moving each day with no chance for drying, the bag soon becomes noticeably moist and less warm. For this reason people in areas that are consistently humid in winter are replacing old down bags—as well as parkas—with polyester.

The most convenient way to dry the bag in winter is to have a bright, warm day that will heat the tent's interior to the 50s or 60s. Wet gear laid out on pads will dry remarkably well this way. If it is possible to dry the sleeping bag and clothing on a sunny day or with a fire, do so. If moisture is a major concern on your winter outing, look into some polyester batting and pile garments. With the vast array of equipment available, there's no reason to sleep cold or carry too heavy a load. And have a backup plan so if the weather is unusually wet and everyone's gear is getting moist, it is possible to end the outing early.

Some planning is necessary to counteract the moisture buildup in clothes and sleeping bags. Most people probably accept it on less than a week's trip, but three things will do a lot toward keeping you warm on a winter backpack.

First, your body rapidly adapts to cold, and by the second or third night you will tolerate the cold with much less discomfort. Second, if the chill is too great to ignore, remove fewer clothes each night for sleeping. Third, eat heartily before sleeping. A large helping of food high in sugar, eaten partway through the evening, does wonders for sustaining body heat. If you still can't sleep due to chill, remember that the old-timers used to winter camp with only a wool blanket and a can of beans.

Winter campers in the Snow Belt's colder places sometimes use a waterproof liner, called a vapor barrier, in their sleeping bags. Use one when temperature and wind chill are so far below zero that you know it's going to be colder than you are equipped for. The liner will keep the insulation in your sleeping bag dry because vapor from your body can't get through to moisten it. Some people believe that keeping the moisture in contact with your body also increases warmth.

A vapor barrier is probably an emergency measure, because the amount of moisture that comes off your body in one night is both amazing and disgusting.

BIGfoot Says ▸▸

Combating moisture is a big factor in surviving winter cold. Prevention makes the most sense. First, move slower and regulate body temperature through layering if your movement is causing too much sweating. Second, protect yourself early from precipitation by using water-proof gear and by setting up camp. Third, understand your limits in equipment and comfort, even if it means turning back.

Any clothing you wear will be soaked by morning, so it's best to sleep nude. A towel is desirable, because you will emerge from the vapor barrier nearly as wet as after a shower and as smelly as an unwashed sock. You might want to try this at home first. The liner is a potential lifesaver for people who enjoy winter camping in the really cold backcountry and something that might be added to emergency equipment for any winter campers.

Most bags have a zipper opening with a hood. The hood is, of course, vital in cold weather and should have a simple drawstring to cinch it down when the zipper is entirely shut, leaving an opening just large enough to breathe through. It is a mistake to breathe inside the bag since your breath is laden with moisture, which will cut the insulating value of the down or polyester. The snorkel—a 6-inch length of wool sock held in place by elastic and used as a breathing tube—is a real help in sleeping; the exhaled air warms the wool, and the inhaled air is thus somewhat warmed. Breathing cold air severely chills the body.

Some otherwise excellent sleeping bags have added gimmicks that cut the warmth considerably. Long zippers tend to be cold, even when special insulation tubes lap over them. Some are designed to be zipped onto another bag to create a double bag for two, but generally these combinations sacrifice warmth and add weight and cost.

Sometimes in winter the tent or snow cave seems confining. Falling snow packs against tent walls, further constricting already tight quarters. Great piles of snow falling out of trees hit the surface with dull thuds that make sound sleep difficult. Wind flaps the tent, adding another irritation. Snowshoers have been known to have nightmares under such circumstances and rip their way out of the sleeping bag with appropriate grunts and snarls. You might want to reconsider why you are out there and your definition of fun.

PACKS

You will need a pack big enough to carry the clothing and extras necessary for a winter outing. A pack with a huge sack is better than a small rucksack jammed so full it is hard to find things. It takes more equipment to hike in the winter than in summer, whether on a one-day hike or overnight. If it is all inside the bag, it won't get as snowy as it will tied on the outside of an undersized pack.

There are many styles of packs with a wide range of prices. The more expensive ones are usually lighter in weight and made of water-repellent nylon fabric. The most valuable qualities are durability (so the pack will not fall apart and require time for repairs), plenty of room inside the main bag (so there will be no need to tie things on the outside), padded shoulder and hip straps (to support weight comfortably), and possibly several outside pockets (for goggles, compass, snacks, water bottles, moleskin, and other frequently used items). In order to protect the contents of the pack in melting snow and rain, use a large plastic bag as a liner, and/or put items in separate plastic bags. Consider a waterproof pack cover for those extra-wet climates.

There are three basic kinds of packs: those with an external frame, those with an internal frame, and those with no frame (soft packs).

The purpose of the **external frame** often made of lightweight aluminum or fiberglass, is to provide a rigid platform for attaching straps and bag. Wide straps hold the frame away from the wearer's body. Shoulder straps attach just above the center of the external or internal frame and again at the lower corners. The hip strap is also attached at both sides of the lower points of the frame. These packs ride high and are not great for heavily wooded areas with low-slung branches.

The most popular are the **internal-frame** packs. On winter day trips, a 2,500- to 3,500-cubic-inch capacity has enough space for extra clothing, food, water, and emergency items. The larger 3,500- to 5,000-cubic-inch capacity works for those weekend trips with a couple of overnights. The largest of the internal-frame models, 5,000 to 6,000 cubic inches or more, will hold enough gear for a week's camping in winter. The cost is often in direct propor-tion to the size, and a person needs to be strong enough to carry it.

The internal frame is simpler and less bulky than the external frame, so the internal frame pack rides closer to the wearer's body. Some external frames extend above your head, others are wider than your body, and some wrap halfway around your hips, making balance more of a problem.

The rigidity of the **soft pack** depends on the way its load is packed. Sleeping bag, clothing, and soft items obviously will claim the side next to the wearer's back to protect shoulder blades and spine from such sharp objects as stove and food containers. The pack rides against your body from hips to neck or above, depending on how much gear you take. Padded shoulder straps and hip strap complete the soft touch against your body. Soft packs have more give and don't abrade the arms the way a frame pack does when you take it off or put it on.

Choose a pack that will do the most things and perform best for you. When snowshoeing in rugged terrain, avoid the medicine show–type pack—with sleeping bag, pots and pans, and camp shoes strapped on the outside and extending above your head. Winter backpacking trips often involve a location where camp is set up and from where campers take day trips. Some people put a small day pack in their large pack to use for the shorter trips, even though the day pack may weigh three pounds or more—nearly as much as the sleeping bag. To save carrying those extra pounds, if possible, find a large backpack that is comfortable and can be used for day hikes. Many packs have compression straps that will compact a large pack for a smaller load during the day.

Proper pack fit makes breathing easier: a heavy load on the shoulders impedes breathing and cuts down on the air supply to the lungs, which in turn slows the flow of nourishment to the blood and increases fatigue. Internal-frame packs can be adjusted to comfortably fit almost any average-size person, but try on different types and sizes. You should be able to shorten or lengthen the shoulder straps to adjust the load so that it is not so tight that the pack bruises your back or so loose that it hangs down on your buttocks. The wide, padded waistbelt should ride on your hip bones just below your belt or waistband. Proper adjustment is when the weight of the pack is carried partly on the shoulder straps and partly on the hip strap, thereby taking the strain off the shoulder muscles.

Whatever pack you choose, learn to pack it, adjust it, and carry it efficiently on whatever terrain you encounter. Make sure that you know how far it sticks up, out, and behind so you don't get stuck in narrow places. Also make sure you can sit down and scoot yourself down a steep incline without the pack forcing you over frontward. (Many trees fall in winter in thick forests and must be climbed over or squeezed under.)

It is also annoying to the rest of the party if one person must constantly stop to adjust shoulder straps, rearrange a hard object, or delve deep into the main compartment to locate a snack—especially when that person has the "Twenty-First Century Special" with nine outside pockets, five zippered compartments, and an extension sleeve on the top that doubles as a bivouac bag in case of a storm. The middle of a snowshoe trail is not the place to out-fumble your companions.

STOVES

Camp stoves have gained importance because wood fires are impractical—and often illegal—for hikers and climbers to use. This restriction is probably more benefit than drawback, because winter forests don't necessarily have large quanti-ties of easy-to-gather dry wood. In fact, as more people use the mountains and backcountry for year-round recreation, the firewood supply in popular places has, for all practical purposes, been used up.

In winter, stoves are used a great deal more than in summer. Usually snow must be melted for water because streams are either deeply buried under snow or are frozen. A stove's quality and functionality take on a great deal more importance, so do extensive research before you purchase one. With the information and suggestions in this section, matched with availability, preferences, and conditions where the stove will be used, you should be able to ask the right questions to find the best equipment. Details of operation, mainte-nance, and parts availability will vary by make and model. Be sure to study the instruction manual and practice using the stove before you go into the backcountry.

The main considerations for winter use are that the stove put out a lot of heat, operate simply, work at high altitude, function well in extreme cold and wind,

stand on a large enough base for stability, and run on fuel that is available in the area. Weight and size are also factors; however, heavy-duty use during winter conditions may require more than the lightest and smallest of stoves.

White gas is the most popular fuel in North America, but harder to find in other places. It is a good winter fuel since it works in cold and at altitude, burns hot and reasonably clean, is not very expen-sive, uses light, reusable containers, and is less likely to emit toxic fumes. White gas stoves need to be pumped, and the gas is its own primer. Spilled white gas evapo-rates quickly. Despite its name, it is a liquid fuel.

Kerosene is another good winter fuel, and is an alternative fuel for some white gas stoves. Kerosene also is good in cold and at altitude, burns hot, needs pumping and priming, but needs to be primed with white gas, alcohol, or lighter fluid. It is not as clean as white gas in burning or mainte-nance. It is less volatile, thus safer to transport.

BIGfoot Says ▶▶
Before choosing a stove consider fuel: Is it available in the area? Is it effective in conditions of cold, altitude, and wind? Is it easy to pump, prime, light, and maintain? What are its burning qualities? What containers are needed for extra fuel? You can get help from your local mountain shops and guide services, but the ultimate choice will be yours.

BIGfoot Says ▶▶

If you plan to travel by air to faraway places, investigate before finalizing your flight plans. Current regulations restrict the transport of stoves, containers, and fuels. Don't take the chance of having your equipment confiscated and/or incurring heavy fines.

Unleaded, low-octane **auto gas** is another alternative for liquid gas stoves. Though readily available, especially in out-of-the-way places, it can change the flavor of your food with a lot of smoke, fumes, and soot. The fumes are toxic so it can only be used outside.

Often more convenient and easy to operate are the gaseous fuel stoves that burn **butane** or **butane/propane blends.** The biggest drawback is these stoves aren't as hot in extreme cold and butane is weaker at high altitude. The fuel needs to be warmed before it can be used. After weighing both sides, these fuels can be considered excellent for moderate conditions.

Propane is a reasonable winter fuel except that the stoves are generally larger and the fuel canisters are quite large and very heavy.

The fuel container should be simple to refill, because fuel requirements in winter are higher than those in summer. For my style of cooking, a quart of white gas is adequate for two people for a week's outing, including melting water from snow. I carry an extra pint of fuel in case we use more. Some people will need twice as much fuel as I use, so be careful not to leave yourself short.

The stove should have a pump so it can be pressurized quickly. Stoves without pumps must be warmed by hand or primed to develop pressure, and warming your cold stove by hand in winter can be unpleasant.

The drawbacks of most stoves are either heavy weight or the need to refill the tank frequently. However, if the cook is careful to top off the tank after the evening meal, it will be all set to go for breakfast. A large tank should last several days, and experience will indicate when the tank needs refilling.

The key to cooking on any stove is planning and getting expert at starting, refilling, repairing, and adjusting the pressure and flame on your stove. This takes practice.

There are many gaseous fuel stoves without pumps that can be used in winter, even in subzero temperatures. Again, planning is the key. The whole stove may need to be warmed inside a parka or sleeping bag before opening the valve. The warming increases the pressure in the tank so the fuel is forced out to the burner when the valve is cracked open.

A firm platform to set the stove on is necessary for stability. If you can't find a flat rock or hard, nonsnowy surface (because snow will melt underneath the stove), carry a square of fireproof foam material in your pack to use as a base. Also among stove accessories should be some sort of folding screen to protect the stove against wind. Other things that you may need include a "pricker" to clean the burner orifice if it carbons up and plugs, and a lot of matches in case your easy-starting "pet" stove becomes reluctant with no warning and there is no backup stove in the group.

Be very careful to keep dirt out of stoves, especially those that must be dismantled for carrying. Check pump leathers and gaskets frequently; they need to be replaced period-ically. Check the manual for other servicing require-ments. Stove failures in winter are likely to be a result of operator error or carelessness.

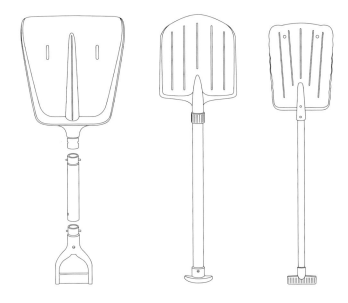

Figure 21. Shovels are a must in avalanche country and for other emergency use.

Now that you have selected your new stove, read the instructions, and practiced—what's for dinner?

SHOVELS

A most useful tool in snow country is the lightweight shovel designed specifically for use in snow (Figure 21). Since every serious backcountry snow traveler should carry one, weight and portability are of great concern. Snow shovels are generally made of sturdy aluminum or unusually hard plastic, with adjustable or detachable handles. The blade needs to be big enough to scoop snow and strong enough to penetrate icy conditions, and the handle should provide good leverage and be comfortable to work with. Plastic blades should be guaranteed by testing that they are not brittle in extreme cold.

As an emergency tool, a shovel is a must to dig out an avalanche victim or build an unplanned overnight shelter. But a shovel can also be useful for making benches or tables for picnics; platforms for tents, stoves, or sleeping bags; and even steps to help you get to somewhere else. Just for fun, hand a shovel to a kid, young or old, and watch: he or she will do something creative with it.

If you plan to build a snow cave or igloo, consider a heavy-duty shovel such as a grain-scoop type to make the job easier; use your lighter shovel for the finish work.

SLEDS

Now that we have talked about all this equipment, let's discuss an alternative to the larger and larger backpack to carry it all: the sled, sometimes called a pulk. For the backcountry, we do not suggest a saucer and rope. Sleds that effectively lighten a load by sliding and control are similar to, but smaller than, the rescue sleds used at ski areas and by mountain rescue groups (Figure 22).

Originally designed to be used with skis, sleds are perfect—even easier—with snowshoes, although they are best pulled using double snowshoe poles. The heavy-duty hulls are molded out of either polyethylene or fiberglass. Aluminum

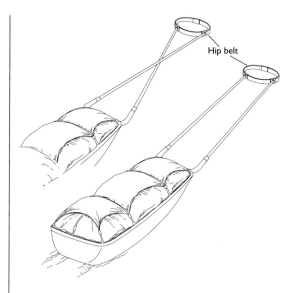

Figure 22. A lightweight sled carries more than twice the load of one expedition-size pack.

> **BIGfoot Says ▶▶**
>
> For a less expensive homemade sled, first buy a kid's sled (the flat type) the size you wouldn't mind pulling. Attach about 9 feet of rope, cord, or web strap to each side front outside edge. Draw the rope through about 6½ feet of PVC pipe on each side and attach it to the waist belt of your pack or tie it around your waist. Put cargo in a plastic bag or in stuff sacks, and secure it with bungee cords to the sled.

runners keep the sled on track, with rudders available for more extreme conditions. Two aircraft-type, adjustable aluminum tubing or fiberglass tow poles extend from the front of the sled up to a padded waist belt, and enable you to pull forward and backward and keep the sled on track, stable on a traverse, and off your heels on the downhill.

Several sled sizes are available, ranging from 3½ feet to 6 feet long and 17 to 18 inches wide, and weighing only 10 to 15 pounds. Under the heavy zippered nylon covers, held closed by compression straps to eliminate sway, the capacity in volume and weight off your back can be

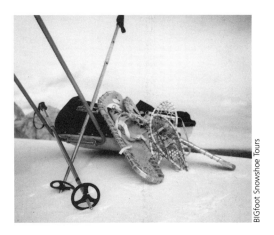

Snowshoes, poles, and sled at rest in the high country

BIGfoot Snowshoe Tours

from two to three times the carrying ability of a 6,000-cubic-inch expedition backpack. For extra pulling capability, shoulder straps can be added.

WATER BOTTLES AND HYDRATION SYSTEMS

Hydration is the best prevention for hypothermia and dehydration, and therefore best for survival (see Chapter 12 for more). The newest method of obtaining necessary fluids is called a hydration system, which consists of a bladder in your pack, a tube to suck it out with, and a mouthpiece that knows when you are not sucking. It is easy, convenient, and almost foolproof, except when cold. The tube can be insulated using special covers from the manufacturer or foam tubing from the hardware store. The mouthpiece will freeze quickly because of exposure. To solve this problem, keep it tucked inside your shirt next to the warmth of your body. Always have at least one spare half-liter bottle in your pack for an emergency refill.

Old-fashioned—yet mostly preferred, convenient, and versatile—is the water bottle. Not the bicycle pop-up spout bottle whose top leaks and freezes, but a sturdy wide-mouth bottle with a screw cap. The wide mouth will not freeze as quickly, and the screw cap won't leak. In extreme cold turn the bottle upside down, since water starts to freeze from the top, and the screw cap threads will freeze last. I keep my water bottles in an old ragg-wool sock for extra insulation and to soak up any drips. Try adding about a quarter to a third of juice to lower the freezing temperature; it will also give you a little sugar boost with each sip. Keep the bottle inside your pack instead of in a side holster on your waist belt, where it is exposed and will get in the way of your double poles. Just remember to drink, drink, drink!

CHAPTER 7

Physical Conditioning

Most people enjoy an activity until they become tired. The more strenuous the activity, the sooner fatigue detracts from enjoyment. Actually, only a few people enjoy snowshoeing for itself. Almost everyone who snowshoes loves the winter outdoors, which offers aesthetic, emotional, or even sensual pleasures. They enjoy the beauty; the sense of being humble in the presence of magnificent mountains; the clean, crisp atmosphere of unspoiled wilderness; and the exultation of reaching a difficult objective. Snowshoes are merely the means of getting out into the natural scene rather than viewing it from a distance.

Physical fatigue not only spoils the fun of an outing but also may create danger by clouding perception and judgment. Tired parties may choose an apparently less strenuous return route only to find that fatigue-influenced shortcuts or alternatives become extremely dangerous or impossible routes.

Realistically, good physical condition is the best safeguard against emergencies. By conditioning you recognize your limits. You are more likely to avoid fatigue-caused errors because your mind is clearer. You will know when it is time to turn back because you have tested yourself and know whether you can make it back. And if you can't, you can start building a shelter so that tomorrow, after some rest, you can start out early.

Even people used to summer backpacking may overestimate their abilities in winter. Snowshoeing is tiring in a number of ways—first, because it is hard to get a snowshoe to bite into the snow as

◀◀ ▲ *Author Gene Prater on windswept slopes near the summit of Mount Whitney in California's Sierra Nevada*

firmly as a lug sole grips the solid dirt or rock of a summer trail. There is some slippage almost every step, even with the best of traction: it's step up two, slide back one. Breaking trail through fresh snow takes a lot of effort as the snowshoe compresses it 6 to 10 inches each step. At times, half a mile an hour on a gentle trail is a fast pace; other times, 3 miles an hour may be possible for several hours.

A day in near-zero temperatures has a numbing effect on people unaccustomed to being outdoors in winter, and gusty winds add another energy drain. Cold plus wind equals wind chill to living flesh and a resultant call on the body to turn up the thermostat. We pay for the winter outing with greater fatigue than for the same outing in the summer.

Not only is footing poor and weather fatiguing, but also the body carries two additional burdens when snowshoeing: the weight carried on the feet and that carried on the back. The British Everest formula suggests that the weight of snowshoes on the feet may be as tiring as carrying a forty-pound pack. And the extra clothing and gear necessary to be comfortable in winter often amounts to twenty-five pounds for a day hike; in summer this weight would be adequate for overnight.

Snowshoeing can put an extra strain on a tendon in front of the hip joint. This tendon lifts the leg, and due to the slightly spraddled stance required to compensate for the width of the snowshoes, it is under unusual strain. The wider the snowshoe, the greater the strain. Compounding the problem is the high leg-lift necessary to snowshoe through deep, soft snow.

It is obvious that on snowshoes, the feet must point in the same direction as the snowshoes, especially if the bindings are good. This makes for strenuous, repetitive motion. By contrast, when hiking on a summer trail it is possible to rest the feet and ankles by changing the direction they point. When hiking cross-country some people go to great lengths to vary their foot position, climbing steep slopes pigeon-toed or splayfooted, or sidestepping, first right side, then left side toward the hill. Most of these techniques are impractical on snowshoes, and the lower legs and ankles can reflect the strain.

Another snowshoe-induced ache that deserves mention is rising on the balls of the feet when going uphill; this tires the calf muscles. However, letting the heel sag down flat on the snowshoe webbing stretches this muscle. Either technique results in some leg fatigue.

Anyone who climbs or hikes each week won't find it as necessary to do as much preconditioning. Late autumn and early winter (while you are waiting for enough snow to snowshoe) is the perfect time to condition muscles, heart, and lungs so that your first snow outing can be made with a minimum of discomfort.

One of the most effective dry-ground conditioners for snowshoeing is to hike on long hilly trails wearing heavy hiking boots and carrying a heavy backpack. If you live in the city or flat country, find stairs in tall buildings or a stadium. Bending over to balance the load and pushing each step comes close to duplicating the stance of the snowshoer struggling through deep snow. There is no need to carry a heavy load on every hike to be effective. Alternate with faster, lighter hikes, then add extra-steep hills once in a while. Adding hiking poles to your trail routine will strengthen your upper body, especially if you prefer to use poles while snowshoeing. Endurance conditioning will be of great value if you are planning a long winter trek, with that extra weight on your back in higher altitudes.

Heavy boots are about as close as you can come to duplicating the effect of snowshoes. Ankle weights have been known to cause more injury than good during trail conditioning, so don't add them. Climbing hills with a heavy load in the pack will condition your body to the type of strain that snowshoeing puts on it, plus the pack forces a slow pace and swaying movement typical of snow travel. The lungs must absorb oxygen into the bloodstream and the heart pumps this energy-producing material to replenish the muscles, while the shoulders are burdened down and the rib cage constricted by the load.

Good conditioning for snowshoeing is a relative thing. Conditioning programs will vary to suit individual ambitions. The dedicated mountaineer and backpacker no doubt trains for a much higher level than

> **BIGfoot says ▶▶**
> Hiking with double poles year-round keeps the upper body in condition, and it takes the strain and weight off the legs, knees, and feet. I don't hike or snowshoe without them. Why be in two-wheel drive in four-wheel-drive country?

the novice who has no extensive background of trail-hiking experience. Some people will never desire more than a level snowshoe hike of a few miles.

Any type of conditioning—jogging, calisthenics, weight training, or other activity—can be tiring for the weak and often boring for the strong. But committing to a conditioning program will make mountain hikes more fun. After you have worked hard and strengthened your body, it will respond to your desires on a snowshoe outing, even when the going is difficult. Endure the conditioning hill so you can enjoy the winter treks.

The following is a fitness program for snowshoers who would like to climb major peaks in winter; it can be scaled down proportionally for lesser objectives.

Twice a week, take a conditioning hike, but not on consecutive days. During this hard hill routine, build up to sixty minutes, then on to ninety minutes, with a good elevation gain on bare ground to develop strength and endurance. When conditioning on snow on a packed trail, allow a little more time to compensate for poor footing. If you are conditioning on snowshoes, you have probably achieved the discipline necessary to do strenuous snowshoeing! Use heavy hiking boots and, depending on your upper-body strength, carry up to 20 to 30 percent of your body weight in your backpack (use rocks and/or containers of water). Build up this weight gradually as your strength increases. Do not descend with a heavy load—knees don't need this much stress on a

BIGfoot says ▶▶

The key to an enjoyable and efficient day hike, snowshoe outing, or even a good day in the workplace, is to start out with a good breakfast. Try to eat your usual menu; don't surprise your system. You can't drive your car far on an empty tank—the body needs fuel, too.

downhill—simply take out some of the rocks. Every once in a while, take no load on an uphill as a "bonus." After two or three weeks, cut down to one of these strengthening hikes a week and make the second hike lighter in weight but longer in length. After another couple of weeks, add a third hike a week that is short and quick (probably as the second hike of the weekend), building toward more strenuous hikes in six weeks or two months.

Variety is important and cross-training helps to strengthen and add balance to those snowshoe muscles. A good aerobic base will make life much easier when the snow gets deep and trails get higher. Here are some additional conditioning exercises you can do.

If it is part of your exercise genre, do some **rock climbing,** especially if there is a desert nearby to provide a change from an all-snow recreation diet. New England and Rocky Mountain climbers have frozen waterfalls and iced-up slabs nearby. Practice some ice climbing. This is good practice in the East since a number of peaks have fun approaches involving bushwhacking and cramponing up slides. Snowshoeing is so

Figure 23. Pedaling uphill "while standing" will work those snowshoe climbing quadriceps and calf muscles. For better traction on really tough terrain, it is wise to remain sitting.

dominantly a leg activity that there is a tendency to let the arms and shoulders just go along for the ride. Use these other activities to keep your upper body in tone, also.

Bicycling will increase strength and endurance, whether it is on long road trips in flat country or mountain biking in the hills (see Figure 23). Many cyclists have discovered that snowshoeing is effective winter cross-training, and vice versa works just as well.

It will become obvious that certain muscles are stressed by snowshoeing. A program of ten minutes a day, or more, of **calisthenics** to strengthen these areas can help you get set for strenuous outings, even though you've never done it before. Calisthenics are especially helpful if you're tied to a desk job. It's a good way to begin

the day if done upon rising in an unheated bedroom. Begin gently and work up to a rigorous routine of curl-type sit-ups, push-ups, side leg-lifts, and toe-raises. Preseason ski conditioning exercises can add to the variety, and a stretching regimen is a must to increase your flexibility.

If you belong to a health club or your company has an exercise room, take advantage of the **weight room** (see photo at right), **training machines** (see photo far right), and **special classes.** The stair-climbing devices have a very high transfer in replicating climbing hills and mountains. Bicycle riding—especially pumping standing up, which is almost exactly the motion of the stair machine—does the same. When fall and winter weather is too wet, cold, or otherwise unspeakably atrocious for hiking or biking, one can retreat to a gym and maintain good snowshoeing condition.

Adjust to what is possible for your age and condition. It doesn't take as long to exercise in a cold room, and it does wonders for warming your chilled body and increasing your tolerance for cold weather. Maybe you'll even develop one of those gorgeous bodies we see in the movies.

The purpose of these suggested programs is to build good hiking and snowshoeing condition and maintain it year-round. It is much less painful to recondition after a short layoff than after a twenty-year period of inactivity. Don't try to do it all at once like an overeager

BIGfoot Fotos

BIGfoot Fotos

The weight room builds strength.

Exercise machines develop endurance.

youngster. If you are forty and haven't done anything very athletic since your teens, be patient. If it took you twenty years to attain the degree of physical deterioration typical of some forty-year-olds, it will take a while to reverse the process. If you suspect some heart trouble or any serious physical weakness, have a complete physical examination before starting a program. Each hunting season finds a few weekend warriors whose enthusiasm far exceeded their capability. So

begin slowly. The carcass you reclaim may, with care, be able to carry you far enough back into the hills to give you a new vision of the loveliness of winter hills and the worthwhileness of making the effort to get out and see them. If you can, envision yourself walking through areas where all evidence of man has been erased by deep snow, enjoying the clean, crisp, sparkling air. There is hope. There is a life to live that is richer and fuller if you can get away from the urban scene.

CHAPTER 8

Walking on Snowshoes

Snowshoeing is basically walking: you just strap on your snowshoes and walk away. But there are two important differences. First, the surface is inconsistent—stable and solid, or hard and slippery, or soft and bottomless—and all movements must reflect the condition of the snow. When traction is poor or position precarious, move very gently, with the flowing, fluid movement of a cat stalking a mouse. Don't lunge or leap from step to step, especially on a steep climb or traverse or when making a kick turn, and don't thrust forward so hard that your snowshoe slips backward. Even on a crust, continue to move more gently than you would on dry ground. Deep traction devices are a great aid, but often there is an icy spot in the

midst of acres of firm snow, and this may cause an unexpected slip. Even the deepest traction does not grip on 4 to 5 inches of powder snow on a crust, where the soft snow on top may be too deep for the traction to cut through to the crust below.

The second difference in walking on snow is that snowshoes are longer, wider, heavier, and more unwieldy than hiking boots. It takes some time to condition leg muscles to the slightly wider stance. When walking slowly you center your weight

◀◀ ▲ *Ski poles and an ice ax are necessary aids for maintaining balance on steep slopes or in soft, deep snow.*

BIGfoot says ▶▶

Beginning snowshoers have a tendency to look down at their feet when they walk. You will adjust to the snowshoes much quicker if you keep your head and eyes up, looking forward and down the trail. You won't be as apt to bump your head on overhanging branches either.

alternately over the right and then the left foot. To thus balance on one foot you must move your upper body first a couple of inches left, then a couple of inches right with each step. Snowshoes emphasize this action. The extra weight on the feet tends to cause the snowshoer to take a longer, slower stride than normal, part of the adjustment to walking on snowshoes without undue fatigue.

When snowshoeing uphill, you need a longer stride because in loose snow it is necessary to step far enough that the new step is not undermined by the previous one, especially if the steps sink 8 inches or so into the snow. Short, choppy steps tend to cause a lunge and an unnecessary slip. The effect on a traverse is that the tail of the forward snowshoe slides into the previous step, and any slip results in some sliding downhill. Usually this is of no consequence, but if the route goes through a narrow slot between two trees, even a slight misstep can dump the unwary into the tree hole below.

Generally an **ice ax** is used as a walking stick on level ground. On hillsides it should be in the hand on the uphill side. Sometimes it is best to lean on the ax just a little on a sidehill to make sure you don't accidentally overbalance. The ice ax is a tool that should be kept sharp. As such, it presents a risk of serious injury. You would be wise to get training in its use before you subject yourself to injury miles from your car.

Ski poles require a little more planning to use efficiently because they are longer than an ax and require more time to place accurately. For level going, never swing the baskets ahead of the feet; actually push on the poles like a cross-country skier, which will help propel you along. Carrying a generous portion of your weight on the poles eases the strain on the legs, and a

Figure 24. Making switchback turns and, at top, toeing straight in one steep pitch

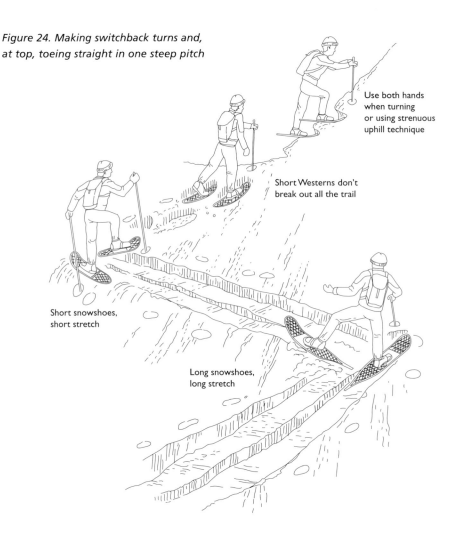

Use both hands when turning or using strenuous uphill technique

Short Westerns don't break out all the trail

Short snowshoes, short stretch

Long snowshoes, long stretch

good high leg lift, necessary for breaking trail in deep, soft snow, is easier to achieve.

The greatest energy-saver, and a vital aid to pacing yourself, is the **rest step,** a momentary pause between steps. With a little practice you can adjust the length of the pause to the state of your fatigue. As you step forward, thrust the front snowshoe out and let it plop down, or stamp it firmly into place. Straighten—lock—your rear knee joint so your tendons and cartilage are holding your weight;

pause and relax your thigh muscles, using the poles or ice ax to maintain balance. Bringing your rear leg ahead, thrust the snowshoe out, place it, lock what is now the rear leg, relax momentarily, and repeat. The effect is to rest the legs during the time they are actually working hard. A couple of seconds of work, a couple of seconds of rest, make it possible to keep going steadily without long stops, during which you have to dig extra clothing out of your pack to prevent chilling. The rest step is a real help when climbing and breaking trail in deep, loose snow, which requires a high leg lift, with special strain on the tendons in the hip area. A brief rest between steps does more good than infrequent, long, sitting-down rests.

The pause during the rest step works to your advantage in loose snow for another reason. The snowshoe is moved forward and stamped down, then after a pause you move gently forward and put your weight on it as the other snowshoe is moved forward and stamped into the snow. By stamping the snowshoe down, you accomplish two things. First, the snow is packed somewhat: even powder snow will firm up—the beginning of age hardening—if there is a pause between placing the snowshoe and putting weight on it. If it is done in one motion without pause, you will sink deeper because it will pack at a greater depth as your full body weight comes down. Second, the snowshoe cuts into the snow and grips it, not only with the traction device, but also with the crosspieces and webbing. Try to pack the

steps at turns and other crucial points.

Take turns breaking trail. In loose snow the trailbreaker may have several extra pounds of snow on his snowshoes. This isn't balled or stuck on; it just falls on top of the webs when he sinks perhaps 8 or 10 inches. Sometimes it is possible to break trail for five minutes continuously when climbing steeply in loose, deep snow; other times it may have to be reduced to as little as two minutes before changing leaders. This system makes it possible for each person to really force the pace for a few minutes while he or she is breaking trail. If there are five people taking turns, each will get twelve minutes of rest between three-minute turns in the lead. As the time for breaking trail ends, the leader steps out of the way and drops to the rear as the rest of the party moves on past.

Most western mountain areas where snowshoeing is popular are different from eastern mountains in snowfall pattern and forest cover. Generally snowfall is heavier, so snowshoers have soft snow to travel on. Second, the westerners ascend ridges in switchbacks carefully engineered to create an inclined plane up which the hikers move steadily and consistently (Figure 24). This is in contrast to that classic section of the Appalachian Trail through Mahoosuc Notch and on up Mahoosuc Arm, which apparently seeks out the hard way.

The more open western forests lend themselves to a switchbacking snowshoe trail. Frequently deep snow hides the real trail, so snowshoers pick their own routes from open space to open space, which doesn't seem to exist in the East. Steep mountain slopes above timberline in the West are frequently wind-packed or firmed up by the sun, so people leave snowshoes off and kick steps in the snow to the summit. Sometimes crampons are handy if an unusually hard crust has developed.

Switchbacking is a pattern that developed in the West after World War II. Probably part of the switchback tradition was aided by the 10 x 56–inch Yukon snowshoes that were so available after the war. The price was right, and if you couldn't find the regular trail everyone understood about switchbacking; the narrow Yukons were good for traversing, but you certainly can't kick steps straight up with those high toes. It is interesting to speculate on what might have happened if any of those flat-toe, super-step-kicking eastern snowshoes or snowshoers had been around to teach us westerners how it's done.

However, the 12-inch-wide eastern step-kicking beavertails had problems on a narrow western traverse and made the 10-inch-wide Yukons look good. A narrow width makes it possible to edge the snowshoe in 3 to 4 inches and continue to climb comfortably. Edging can be simply kicking the snowshoe sideways into the slope (Figure 26), or moving the boot heel as far toward the uphill side of the slope as possible, then stamping down and forcing the edge of the snowshoe into the slope.

In the late 1960s I further modified a 10 x 36–inch modified bearpaw by moving the hinge and binding far forward. This provided the prototype for the present Western snowshoes: it created a shoe that was narrow for traversing and also had a flat toe for excellent step kicking. Today's smaller Western models are used as an extension of bare-boot climbing on firm spring snow: the extra flotation provided by the snowshoe makes this early spring climbing possible in January or February rather than in May.

The typical Western snowshoe as it eventually evolved has a high toe, 3 to 5 inches. Western step-kicking technique requires soft snow, but instead of kicking

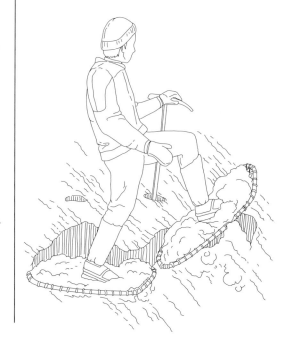

Figure 25. Traversing steep, deep snow requires an extremely high lift of the uphill leg.

through a crust the snowshoe is more often stomped down to pack a step (Figure 27). Frequently, switchbacks are nearly straight up the slope rather than the gentle angle shown in Figure 24.

The high toe works well in two situations. First, it is easier to pull up out of deep, soft snow when ascending a slope, because it rides up rather than burrowing under as a flat toe does. Second, it also pulls out of deep snow when descending by plunge stepping or simply walking on the level. The high toe kick-steps adequately in soft western snow, although the flat toe is much better for eastern crust. Generally, western snow is softer than the crusted snow in the East, so the high toe is preferred in the West.

Snowshoers in British Columbia use the same western switchback technique, but their soft powder snow dictates a larger snowshoe. A 9 x 34– to 9 x 36–inch Western and the 10 x 36–inch Green Mountain with forward-mounted bindings are large enough to give adequate flotation, yet short enough to be maneuverable and still kick steps. Frequently, a smaller snowshoe would be large enough, if it weren't for the hoarfrost around boulders, stumps, and any other object sticking up in the snow. Cold temperatures create this zone of unstructured crystals around these objects. This may be to British Columbia what spruce traps are to New England: the 3-foot-long snowshoe is the minimum length to keep from falling into the hoar. In May, when the snow gets firmer, smaller snowshoes are more practical.

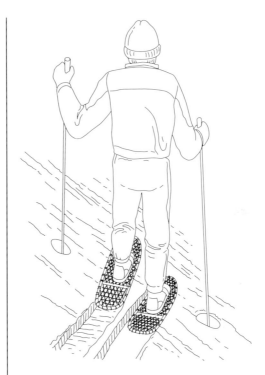

Figure 26. Edging with narrow Western snowshoes in snow that is firm but not crusted

Some suggestions on switchbacks and step kicking may be of help to beginners who are unfamiliar with these techniques. Usually ascend at a grade a little less than the maximum angle the snowshoes will climb (the maximum angle of course requires that you hang on with great effort, always on the verge of slipping, and is very tiring). Use an angle of ascent that is comfortable and lets you relax somewhat. At the point of turning, for example to the right, plant the left snowshoe firmly and stamp it in so it will hold. If you are using an ice ax, place it in the slope above the binding of the left snowshoe and work it in securely. Ski poles should be planted below the snowshoes, alongside the boot heels (Figure 24). Then shift weight to the left snowshoe and ax or poles, face the slope, swing the right snowshoe around to point it in the direction the next switchback will take, and shove it into the snow. Make sure you place the right snowshoe so the tail is not on the left snowshoe. Stamp the right web into the snow and gently shift weight and step on it. Try to stay well above your previous trail, which has undermined the snow you are now building the turn on. Reverse the procedure to make a left turn.

The very short, narrow, aluminum-frame snowshoes allow a modified technique. The 8 x 25–inch model, for example, requires merely that you kick steps as you would when snow climbing without snowshoes. These webs are so small that they do not interfere as seriously with the placement of your feet on turns.

As each succeeding snowshoer uses the turn, the trail shoulders may slough off and latecomers may have a harder time getting around than the leader. By all means use special care in placing snowshoes precisely where they were placed before, widening and deepening the tracks for those who follow. Special care in placing snowshoes, ice ax, or poles will pay dividends in avoiding slips. Sometimes

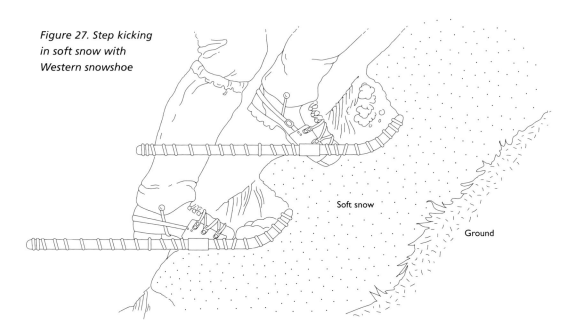

Figure 27. Step kicking in soft snow with Western snowshoe

Soft snow

Ground

there is only one way past an obstacle. Be sure to preserve the trail so others following do not have to rebuild it.

There are other ways to make the snowshoe turn easier. Plan to use the gentlest places on a slope for the turns; look ahead and pick the route to use the terrain to your advantage. Avoid the steepest parts and don't hesitate to make short switchbacks between main turns. Use trees and their branches for handholds.

Figure 28. Traversing with large snowshoes usually develops two trails, one above the other.

When the snow is soft enough, the trail can be two snowshoe widths wide and relatively level, but often the snow is too firm for that and requires one snowshoe trail slightly above the other (Figure 28). People on 36-inch and shorter snowshoes have an advantage in this situation as these shorter snowshoes may be placed one ahead of the other. This keeps the feet at the same height (Figure 29), which is less tiring than the two-trail technique. Beavertails overlap some and can be used almost single file, but still are at a disadvantage compared to the 8-inch width on sidehills.

Balance is critical when placing one snowshoe ahead of the other. Ordinarily the feet are spaced far enough apart for good stability. But traversing with the snowshoes single file decreases stability, so the poles or ice ax must compensate. A person with short snowshoes may save some effort on a traverse, but will do so at the expense of irritating someone in the group who is wearing long Yukons.

Another benefit of using shorter snowshoes with forward-mounted bindings is their practicality for kicking the toes in and climbing straight up a steep pitch (step kicking). This technique is strenuous and requires soft snow, so it is limited to short pitches. Long slopes with enough soft snow to kick the toes in for a good step could also be steep and unstable enough to avalanche. (See Chapter 11, and under those conditions, stay in the trees, the outside edge of the open areas, or look for a safer slope, if at all possible.) The method is to swing the snowshoe backward and flip the tail up. The toe is kicked straight into the slope, with the web horizontal and the tails sticking out in the air. The forward-hinged 36-inchers and shorter shoes work well for this; a strong snowshoer can use the larger shoes, too, although it is more difficult. Obviously the snow must be right—soft enough to kick the snowshoe in 12 to 16 inches and still firm enough to support the snowshoer.

Long steps, spaced wider apart laterally, are necessary for this straight-up technique, because the lower step, deep as it needs to be, badly undermines the step above. Steps such as these are weak and do not form a trail adequate for a large party. The main use of this technique is along ridges, where drifting creates slopes too steep to angle up and without enough room to switchback around the obstruction. With more skill and practice you will find other places where a short, steep pitch climbed straight up may save time. Although admittedly of limited use, this technique is one more way to save energy over a long pull.

Techniques such as the kick turn and toeing in straight up are easier if you can extend your legs and take long steps, placing the forward snowshoe in undisturbed snow that has not been undermined by other steps. Movements must be smooth and precise, which may be a little too much for the untrained muscles of beginners, when fatigue begins to build up and overextended muscles begin to protest.

The eastern step-kicking technique was developed for eastern conditions, which

Figure 29. Short snowshoes allow a single-file traverse.

include crusted snow, steep slopes, dense forests, and local trail habits. Snowfall in the White Mountains of New Hampshire is about half the average in the Cascades. The January—or December or February—thaws are caused by moist air from the Atlantic Ocean or Gulf of Mexico moving inland, pushing cold air out and dumping rain in this normally frigid area.

Rain on the cold snow may not penetrate more than an inch or two. Arctic air from Canada immediately repossesses the land, and the return to zero guarantees a quick-frozen hard crust. Often there is powder snow underneath. The crust is too hard to edge a snowshoe into, too weak to bare-boot it, so when it gets too steep to snowshoe-crampon up it, you sink the ice ax or pole tips in for stability and start driving the toes of your snowshoes through it (Figure 30)—and hope you don't splinter the toe of your snowshoe frame against a granite stone just under the surface. Modern aluminum frames can take more surprise abuse.

On hard-packed slopes, such as sturdy wind slab and spring or sun-hardened snow, there is no step kicking or sidestepping through the hard surface. The shorter modern snowshoes with their built-in aggressive crampon-type claws are the only way to go. Under these conditions, it is

more efficient to go straight up the "fall line," planting as much claw into the hard surface as possible while pushing up the hill with ski poles placed at a comfortable balance point. This can be very strenuous if you try to go too fast, but puts less strain on legs and ankles during switchback traverses (see photos on page 118).

For a short traverse around a rock, tree, or snow dune, again face straight up the fall line and sidestep around the obstacle (as shown in the photos at right) with the snowshoe and pole placement in balance.

Downhill fun is not just for skiers. Fresh powder can be just as enticing for those not carving turns. All that work going up will

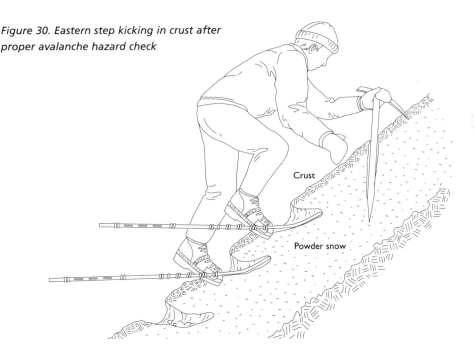

Figure 30. Eastern step kicking in crust after proper avalanche hazard check

Crust

Powder snow

be worth it when you get to those soft downhill sections. The beginning snowshoer may look down the slope with a sense of fear; but with a few pointers, it can be easy and fun. It just takes practice and is much more stable with poles.

The first tendency is to lean forward by bending at the waist, but this leads to a

Photos © Malcolm Stephens

Straight up the hill is the most efficient movement on firm or hard-packed snow.

Running downhill is fun.

Sequence at right: For a short steep traverse, sidestep while facing up the hill for balance.

Photos © BIGfoot Snowshoe Tours

Editor Dave Felkley in a downhill "gallop"

Felkley finishes his gallop with a wild "ee-haw!"

greater chance of face plants. The opposite stance, to lean back as if digging in the heels for brakes, will make it too easy for your snowshoes to slide out from under you. The safest position is straight up, balancing your body directly over the foot, slightly bending your knees to compensate for changes, then relaxing. Unlike those visions of skiers flying down steep slopes, sliding on snowshoes in powder is only for a brief moment and a few inches at a time. If you relax and steady yourself over the snowshoe, you ride right into the next step, with poles assisting in the balance. The experienced snowshoer will use the poles to push more slide into each downhill step.

For the experienced and strong snowshoer to have a little extra fun on short powdery downhills, try an aggressive "galloping" motion. It could best be described as almost a musical waltz beat of step, step, leap … step, step, leap … repeat, repeat. Following a forward leap while pushing off with your poles, land with one snowshoe, then the other about a half length ahead of the first. Then push off with another leap, getting as much forward air or "flying" as far as comfortable. You will always lead with the same foot, whichever side becomes most efficient. It is fast and strenuous, but fun (see photos above)!

Photos © Malcolm Stephens

Aid balance by using a telemark ski position when sliding down steep hills.

Let kids play on snowshoes and they will want to do it again.

A tendency for beginners on the downhill is to want to sidestep as if on the traverse uphill. If the slope is not too steep and the snow is of the right consistency to make steps, this can be done. However, when gravity and fresh powder want to move the snowshoer straight down the hill (called the "fall line" in skiing), point the snowshoes in that way for more control. Ride each step with one snowshoe out front, then take another riding step with the other. This action is similar to the telemark ski position without the turns (see photo above right).

When the snow is not so soft and fluffy, downhill technique needs to rely more on the traction devices under the foot, while using the tips of the poles and/or a sharp-pointed ice ax for additional balance and grip. It may be harder to relax under conditions of extra-firm snow, or especially icy crust, but it is still important to stay centered over the snowshoe claws. If trees are nearby, check out the snow there: it could be much softer, therefore easier on your knees.

Snowshoeing can be fun for kids of all ages. My grandson started at age three and grandpa still takes folks on snowshoe tours. The secret for everyone is to learn to play. The younger the snowshoer, the more important it is to not really have a destination, or at least one not very far. Keep the activity short in time and radius from your starting point. Keep it easy and

BIGfoot Snowshoe Tours

Boys running at end of a snowshoe tour

playful so the experience will make kids want more. Until becoming more adult in size and strength, the youngsters don't need poles—with such a low center of gravity, poles just get in their way. Adults should be close by to get them up after

falls in deep powder, but remember that it is difficult to get hurt in soft snow.

As you travel more on snow it will become apparent that patience is necessary to enjoy winter travel. You can't race in, see the view, and sprint out; it's too difficult to move fast on snow. Also, during winter there are fewer daylight hours. Take time to enjoy the trip—make the scenery along the way as much a goal as the destination. Patience also means not getting upset by minor equipment problems and changes of plan. A broken strap or loose rivet is never convenient to repair, but it should be fixed before it becomes a major breakage. Be sure to get camp set up in time to get adequate rest. Realize that snow is inconsistent and revise your schedule if necessary. Take time to avoid possible avalanche areas (see Chapter 11). Do a good job of route finding, trail-breaking, and camping, and if necessary give up an objective if the danger from storm or avalanche is too great. The penalty for error in the winter is much greater than it is in the summer.

CHAPTER 9

Snow Conditions

Snow is at all times sensitive to an infinite variety of modifying conditions. The only predictable thing about it is that it will be different higher up, around the corner, or over the ridge. Temperature and wind are the determining factors. Cold temperatures are associated with powder snow. A crusted condition results from changing temperatures: warming and thawing melt the surface, then cold temperatures freeze it. The areas that have warmed the most will refreeze, pack, and become the most firm. Generally the temperature is colder at higher elevations, dropping approximately 3°F with each additional thousand feet.

North sides of mountains, deep shaded valleys with heavy timber, and lee slopes that collect windblown snow are the slowest to firm up. North sides of mountains and lee slopes also have the hazard of avalanches the longest.

Where the wind blows, nature's sculpting flows; from waving cornices to high piled dunes, her artistic sense sure shows. While studying these snow conditions, take time to notice and appreciate the snow, ice, and windblown formations—from snowflakes to ice crystals, from snow dunes to cornices—and the artistic swirls of beauty from Mother Nature.

Wind does two things. It packs and therefore firms areas where it blows constantly. Wind pack has the same effect on powder snow as increased temperature and is an advantage to winter travel. Snow falling in wind usually forms wind slab, an adverse effect of wind that will be discussed more fully with avalanches (Chapter 11). Wind slab can be on lee slopes, where much windblown snow has drifted in, or on areas that face the wind if the new snow is

◀◀ ▲ *Winter snowshoe ascent of Mount Daniel in Washington's Cascades* not packed and consolidated with the underlying snowpack. Either circumstance may form an extremely unstable condition.

The force of gravity is another factor modifying the behavior of snow on slopes of mountains or hills. A fresh, stable deposit of snow, when sufficiently warmed by the sun, may begin to flow like water and avalanche into the valley bottom. Or the wind may blow certain areas free of snow, depositing it in extra-deep layers in sheltered locations.

The textbook set of snow conditions in the **Cascades** is slush in the valley bottoms with powder snow on the upper slopes and variations of both in between. However, conditions seldom follow the pattern exactly because forest, cloud cover, wind, and direction of slopes create microclimates.

For example, a fresh snowfall may remain powdery until storm clouds pass and the sun comes out. Then sheltered,

BIGfoot says ▸▸

In those warmer days of snowshoe travel, think of rain, if it happens, as immature snow!

open south slopes may become slushy from valley floor to ridge top on a warm afternoon, freezing at night into an iron-hard crust. A thick stand of tall evergreens just above the valley bottom may shelter powder snow for several days after the storm has passed and temperatures have warmed, yet snow melting off the trees may refreeze under each tree into an icy patch surrounded by powder. North slopes may not warm up for weeks at a time, and so have deep powder most of the winter. Ridge tops cooled by constant wind do not develop crust, yet may be wind-packed hard as ice. Nearby may be a patch of powder cooled by the wind, yet on the side facing the sun, or there may be slush on the lee side of a clump of trees, sheltered from the wind and warmed by the sun.

Knowledge of local conditions and routes that are avalanche-free is very important. Sometimes cold temperatures, powder snow, and the short daylight hours of January and early February effectively limit snow travel to foothills and nearby destinations. With firmer snow and longer days later in winter, you can get to the lower viewpoints in a few hours and more distant peaks are reasonable objectives.

Colder mountain ranges do not experience the cycle of new snowfall/warming and settling/new snow/warming as often as the Cascades, which have a marine climate. Some generalizations may be made on snow condition and temperature pattern, but not about specific avalanche hazard in a given area. Avalanche hazard must be determined in the field, at each location, and in person (see Chapter 11).

The **Rocky Mountains** of both the United States and Canada, the **Interior Ranges** of British Columbia, the **Wasatch** in Utah, and the **Sierra** of California have certain similarities due to their cold temperatures. Mid-December to mid- or late January frequently sees the record minimum temperatures. There are usually several feet of snow on the ground by this time. Severe subzero Fahrenheit readings cause depth hoar buildup within or at the bottom of the snowpack, which creates a great avalanche hazard. (Depth hoar is discussed in Chapter 11.)

Powder snow in these ranges generally lasts from mid-November to mid-February or mid-April. This depends on weather patterns, as spring arrives earlier some years than others. In these mountain areas the favorite snowshoes are the larger Western styles or 10 x 36-inch Green Mountain with forward-mounted binding, because hikers generally avoid the period— the first few days after snowfalls—in which even larger models would be needed. This is due to the extreme avalanche hazard during and after snowfalls, which often can be several feet per storm. Hikers and climbers in these rugged mountain areas must have firm snow for safety and reasonable traveling conditions. Later in spring, when the snow is really firm, some backpackers use the smaller Westerns.

In the **Anchorage,** Alaska, area even the larger Westerns are a little small some winters since heavy snowfall and cold temperatures prolong deep powder snow. In the interior, such as **Big Delta,** the largest snowshoes can sink more than knee deep. Sled dog racers on the Anchorage-to-Nome 1,200-mile Iditarod race may want those larger models when bucking deep powder.

The **Wyoming/Montana** areas are regarded by the locals as the coldest in the Lower 48, with a record low of –63°F in the high-elevation Jackson Hole/Yellowstone plateau area. The coldest period is during late December to mid-January. Snow is powder, with not much before Christmas; storms build it deeper without much base until late winter. Depth hoar formation is

High-altitude "sharks" along the Ten Mile Range (peaks above 13,000 feet) near Breckenridge, Colorado

extensive. By March the snow is firm for good traveling. The 6,000-foot-high valleys in this area record the lowest minimums, but also warm up the fastest in the spring and on bright sunny days.

Heaviest snowfall is on the west side of the **Tetons, Wind Rivers,** and the many ranges in **Montana** and **Idaho.** Most of the storms that drop snow in the western ranges originate on the Pacific Ocean. Heavy snowfall with wind is common and creates severe slab avalanche hazard extensively during the winter.

The Rockies and other ranges of **Colorado** have a somewhat similar overall pattern of snow conditions and weather. The coldest temperatures are usually the last week of December and early January. Depth hoar formation is extensive. Despite these conditions there is a strong snowshoeing tradition in the north Colorado Rockies. Deep powder persists in sheltered and forested areas. Large areas above timberline are usually firmer. When avalanche danger is high, activity shifts to lesser peaks (there are 130 peaks higher than 11,000 feet in Colorado). Keep in mind, Colorado has the highest number of reported avalanches of any state.

The more southern areas of the Snow Belt, such as in Colorado and to the south, experience much more sun and clear weather in late winter, which tends to firm up the snow, especially on south-facing slopes in these high, cold ranges. Late winter does not see an end to heavy storms, as March and April normally have very heavy snowfall with wind. By late spring— April or so—there may be a crust on the snow in places, so you can bare-boot it. The San Juans in southwest Colorado and the western side of the Rockies probably have some of the heaviest snowfall. Near Wolf Creek Pass in southern Colorado, low temperatures can reach –50° F.

Utah's **Wasatch** Mountains have somewhat the same snow conditions as the Rockies. Cold weather begins in late October or November. There is usually snow in the mountains when temperatures reach the lowest minimums, in late December and January, with –20° F to be expected and the record around –35° F. These low temperatures and heavy snowfall guarantee a lot of powder snow through the winter. Snowfall is usually accompanied by wind with significant slab avalanche hazard.

There may not be as strong a tradition of early snowshoeing in the Wasatch as in other places in the United States, but it is growing fast. Some people feel that before mid-February it is too cold, and snow travel is easier on firmer snow later in the winter.

The wind blows snow into deep drifts on Caribou Hill (10,500 feet) near Nederland, Colorado.

The elevation of the valleys is from 4,500 feet, with smaller summits up to 8,000 feet, where there are seemingly less avalanche-prone routes.

The main Wasatch Mountains, with summits around 12,000 feet, are rather strenuous for the casual snowshoer and more in the class of the Tetons for winter ascents. Clear weather and bright sunshine make daytime temperatures considerably above nighttime lows. By April, conditions may rapidly change from winter to spring, especially on south-facing slopes.

The **Sierra Nevada** share some similarities to the other high ranges mentioned, particularly that winter normally brings powder snow in generous amounts. Subzero temperatures cause formation of depth hoar, with its long-term avalanche hazard. The coldest temperatures are in the high, over-6,000-foot elevation of northern Owens Valley around Bridgeport, California. There are drought years with little snow, but December, January, and February are the traditional times of deep powder. Snow falls with wind, so the steep slopes are most dangerous. In late winter and spring there are probably longer intervals between storms.

The Sierra range is much farther south than the Montana Rockies, so clear days without wind can bring some thawing and freezing to firm up snow. However, the heaviest snowfall may occur in March, April, and May, which causes a spring snow avalanche hazard in addition to the depth hoar problem.

Mid-February may see firm snow for good travel on lower mountains, with fewer avalanche-prone routes. March and April may see good conditions on the higher peaks, but this depends entirely on weather patterns in any given year, because the snowfall pattern is so changeable from one year to the next. Snowshoes may be used through May in places. The change from summer to winter is one of the greatest hazards. Hikers who are accustomed to the extreme summer heat often get caught by winter temperatures and snowfall, which may occur as early as September or October, or as late as November or December.

The **San Gabriel, San Bernardino,** and **San Jacinto** Mountains south of the Sierra Nevada also have snowshoeing and touring. These summits of 10,000 to 11,500 feet have all the hazards of more northern mountains. Powder snow firms up more rapidly, but temperatures drop to subzero at high elevations and avalanche hazard is present. The smaller Western snowshoes are becoming the favorites in both the Sierra and the San Gabriels.

Large wood-frame snowshoes, such as the Cree or Ojibwa, are the favorite for gentler terrain west of the **Great Lakes.** Powder snow is abundant because of the normal subfreezing and subzero temperatures all winter, until mid-March or so.

The area from Minneapolis–St. Paul north to the iron ranges at Hibbing, Minnesota, features deep powder plus wind. The record minimum of −47°F combined with wind means extreme cold for winter campers. Snow in open areas and on lakes become wind packed, which makes for easier traveling in this area. North of the iron ranges there is less wind, and in these areas snow may remain dry and powdery all winter. Conditions vary tremendously, and sometimes a crust will form. Northern Wisconsin and Michigan's Upper Peninsula can expect deep snow, 6 to 8 feet, so until the snow firms up in this area the largest snowshoes travel best.

In the **East,** expect powder snow with no base by New Year's Day. More snowfalls of powder followed by a thaw and refreezing

Photos by BIGfoot Snowshoe Tours

The wind is always a factor in the high country—watch the sky.

Old trees, shadows, and swirls mixed with blowing snow create winter sculptures.

puts icy layers in the snowpack, with powder in between. High winds above tree line sweep any snowfall to lee sides, causing avalanche hazard. Many of the slides—for example, Jefferson Slide, Adams Slide, and the more publicized Tuckerman and Huntington ravines on New Hampshire's Mount Washington—frequently avalanche. Rime ice buildup creates a need for boot crampons above tree line. There is a similarity between terrain above tree line in the East and the last 500 feet of Mount Rainier in Washington, which is also subject to rime ice buildup called sastrugi. A cloud cap on Rainier indicates high winds inside the cap. The same is true in New Hampshire; clouds on the ridges indicate

high winds above tree line. After the sap starts running in March the snow gets slushy on the lower elevations, and it is time to start rock climbing.

To meet the great variety of conditions found in the mountains, you need to know which snowshoe works best on varied terrain (see Chapter 2). Don't be tempted to get a Yukon on the theory that deep snow is the only problem in the mountains. First of all, the snowshoe must be used on sidehills, making narrow width of prime importance. When more than 2 feet of snow falls, the trail ledge on sidehills begins to disappear. On the level, 3 or 4 feet will hide blazes on trees; 6 to 8 feet will be above the limbless section of trailside trees. Even sections of road drift over and develop formidable slopes that descend steeply to the valley floor in midwinter. If an otherwise simple route crosses a creek and there are 4 feet or more of snow on the ground, it will be a struggle to get down one side and up the other unless you have a shovel and snowshoes designed and equipped to climb well. Trees on sidehills have deep wells—holes in the snow around the trunks—that must be detoured around, perhaps on steep slopes. Fallen trees and drifts on gentle sidehills can create short, steep slopes on otherwise easy hikes. And the mountaineer on the ridge tops is often following a narrow path beside cornices and over drifts.

An 8-inch-wide snowshoe can be edged if the snow is not too hard, but not nearly as effectively as a climbing boot or ski. Wider snowshoes, of course, are just that much less effective. Bindings are too flexible to really "hammer" even narrow snowshoes into hard snow on a sidehill. The nearly straight frames on some models hold better than the curving sides of the bearpaw and beavertail.

Long spells of subzero temperature will freeze even fast-moving mountain streams. This can be a real help by eliminating the problems of crossing unbridged streams. A solidly frozen stream can sometimes

BIGfoot says ▶▶
If there is any question about safe conditions—*DON'T GO!* Try another route, or use your poles to check the conditions. If your poles easily poke through, so will you.

BIGfoot says ▶▶
As snow melts in the spring, oil residue rises to the surface on well-used snowmobile tracks. Remember that oil floats on water, so it will end up on your snowshoes.

shorten a route that has a long trail approach or can eliminate some bushwhacking. However, be extremely careful when crossing any stream on ice, as it frequently is anything but solid and is full of air pockets.

At subzero temperatures flowing water may freeze and block the channel. The water may find a different route under snow. There often is water on top of the ice in a lake solidly frozen. Look for depressions in the snow around the edges of a lake as these may indicate a spring flowing into the lake, creating thin ice at that spot. Falling into water at zero temperatures is quite dangerous, so check thickness of ice before walking out on a frozen stream or lake.

There isn't space to describe all the possible weather patterns and snow conditions in all the snowshoeing areas in the United States and Canada. Reading about it here won't guarantee that you will recognize the dangers described when you are actually in an area new to you. The best this information can do is point out that an outing in a different place can really be great, but you should get some local expert to advise you and help you realize that equipment perfect in one area may not be so great elsewhere.

CHAPTER 10

Route Finding

A glistening snow cover mantling the winter landscape is a thing of magic, giving mountain and hill country such an allure that more and more people each year are drawn to explore its beauty. However, reaching a goal presents an unaccustomed problem in winter. In summer, even distant backcountry can be reached by trails, since the main problem in trail route finding is choosing the proper fork at junctions. Storms and bad weather have relatively little effect on this type of route finding, and maps and trail guides are usually adequate reference material.

Deep snow changes all this by covering not only the trail, but also trail signs, blazes on trees, and even trailside shelters. In heavy timber there is frequently a lane through the trees, but in more open

◀◀ ▲ *Climbing above valley fog in Washington's eastern Cascades*

BIGfoot says ▶▶
Cookie crumbs and snowshoe tracks don't always work to find your way back home. Read on to learn more realistic options.

country all trail signs disappear. In places exposed to wind and drifting snow, such obvious features as roads disappear altogether. Ridge tops are changed the most; drifts 20 or 30 feet high alter the visual aspect of the landscape, and knolls may appear where gullies were in the summer. Some of these changes are for the better, as a great deal of brush and garbage is buried, and some gullies are filled with snow, leveling out a depression or making easy creek crossings where wading was required in summer.

The snowshoer's problem is similar to that of the summer backcountry traveler who goes beyond the trails: choosing a route through obstacles such as cliffs, stream gorges, and impassable thickets. But rather than route finding by trail junctions, the snowshoer looks for topographical features, such as the places where two streams or canyons meet, and relies on other landmarks instead of counting mileposts. A major problem with this method is identifying side canyons or tributary streams. Questions arise as to whether the side canyon you are looking at is the one shown on the map. It is difficult visualizing terrain by interpreting the convoluted contour lines on a map. Frequently trees will totally hide a very obvious tributary stream or valley.

In rugged mountain terrain with high ridges and deep valleys, route finding is fairly simple. It is obvious when a ridge is crossed. There is, however, a lot of travel through forested country where major peaks are hidden by trees or winter clouds, or where, as in the Midwest, there are no peaks. Many winter travelers are familiar with the country; they follow compass courses in summer and plan to do the same in winter. Competent navigation by map and compass has certain advantages over using visual points of reference.

Rather than go into a detailed course in orienteering here, I will use the simplest, most basic method of setting and following a **compass** course to a single objective.

Place the section of map you are using on a level spot, such as a pack with no magnetic items inside—camera, knife, and so on—with the compass on it. When the compass needle stops swinging, align the north-south grid lines of the map with north on the compass. Plot your course on the map. As you travel, you can then use magnetic north without adjusting for the local declination.

Select an object or point to be reached on the map, for instance a stream junction a mile or so away. A direct line across the center of the compass to that point on the map should provide a true bearing to follow. With the map removed, but with the compass oriented as before, sight across the compass at the same reading. The stream junction will be out that direction, a mile or so away.

If you are traveling alone, pick an easily identifiable object along the intended path and proceed to that point. If you are part of a group, send a person to the farthest point you can see on that line, and when he or she is at that point sight to make sure he is still on the compass line. This person then uses his compass to align the next person on the next most distant visible point, and so on.

To check the distance traveled, allow 34 steps of average length on the level for a distance of 100 feet. Use fewer steps for long steps downhill and more for short steps uphill. Measure the mileage on the map and make an approximation by tallying the distance between sightings with the compass. This must be written down, since there are about 53 hundred-foot sightings at the 34-step average in a mile, or 1,802 strides. Before using this method under actual conditions give it a lot of practice. Remember, this method gives you only an estimate; in mountain country, it may even be less accurate.

Be sure that following a compass course is appropriate to the terrain. Steep mountain country with deep canyons or ravines and high ridges is not the best place to set a compass course directly to the objective. In more level country it is easier to navigate directly across streams and divides. In steeper country it may be more appropriate to set a compass course through thick timber to a place, for example where a valley has some gentle slopes to climb to cross a ridge. A course change would be necessary when reaching the point where you begin ascending the side of the ridge. At the ridge top, it might be necessary to set a course into the next valley, perhaps toward a good stream crossing. It takes practice to follow a compass course rapidly and accurately.

For more information, check the navigation section of *Mountaineering: The Freedom of the Hills* (see Suggested Reading) or some references on orienteering. Some skill in navigation techniques is essential when traveling by compass in forested and rugged backcountry.

Although it is desirable to be able to see where you are going, especially in new country, it is best to be so familiar with the area that you are able to recognize small landmarks if the weather is cloudy and major landmarks are hidden. The key is preparation. Choose winter objectives you have been to in summer, or make certain there is someone in the group who knows the area. Not all trail signs are hidden, but it takes an observant person to discern a blaze on a tree down a hole where sheltering branches have created a depression in the snow around the trunk, a limb that has obviously been chopped or sawed

From Algonquin Peak in the Adirondacks' High Peak Region, looking toward Mount Marcy

off, or a section of Forest Service phone line almost hidden in the snow. Study the summer trails and note their location in regard to features that will show clearly in winter, so that if you lose a trail you can continue and pick it up farther on.

One danger in mountain country is potential avalanche slopes or chutes. The 15-minute (1 inch equals about 1 mile) U.S. Geological Survey quad maps that show forest cover give a hint of possible locations of avalanches, such as contour lines that indicate a steep slope in an area without forest cover. The 7 $\frac{1}{2}$ series is even more helpful because of the additional detail of contour lines. U.S. Forest Service maps are of no help in this, nor do summer hiking and climbing guides generally provide such information, and some summer trails cross or ascend slopes that frequently avalanche in winter. Observe the route carefully for avalanche chutes, recognizable as gullies swept clear of trees and leading unobstructed from valley floor to ridge-top snowfields. Stay out of these potential funnels; the snow above may be unstable and avalanche down the gully, so do not hesitate to change your planned route from an open gully to a forested slope. If you snowshoe in areas where avalanches are possible, you should learn the danger signs (see Chapter 11).

The easy part of route finding is getting to the objective—a viewpoint, a mountaintop, or a snow-covered meadow beside a stream. Like summer hikers, snowshoers are inclined to relax when following the return trail; indeed, it is usually as obvious as a summer trail. But in windswept areas take extra precautions, for a change in weather can create conditions that make returning extremely difficult unless the route is marked by brightly colored plastic flagging tied on trees, or by bamboo wands (garden stakes 2 or 3 feet long with flag attached) that may be carried along and placed in open treeless areas. Flags and wands should be picked up on return and carried out. It may be hard to be serious about marking what in clear weather is an obvious route, but clouds and storms can eliminate even a prominent set of tracks and obscure the landscape so that each clump of trees, each ridge or draw looks exactly like every other one. On a clear day the snowshoe trail appears as a slash across each open spot, but a few minutes of blowing snow can obliterate it. In cloudy conditions even flagging and wands are not too effective unless they are very close together or you have recorded compass bearings for the return trail. Even the huge cairns marking trails on Mount Washington in New Hampshire are hard to find in a whiteout, a condition that occurs when clouds merge with blowing snow and all landmarks are hidden.

The simplest method of taking a compass bearing back down the trail for your return is as follows: face in the direction you will be traveling; place the compass a safe distance from any magnetic object, such as exposure meter, watch, ice ax, and so on (a good place is on your mittens laid on the snow); and let the needle stop swinging. Line up north on the compass with the north end of the needle. Sight across the compass from the point where you are toward the direction you want to return. Record this figure.

This is all that an amateur needs to know to get across an unmarked area where visibility is poor. Greater expertise is required if there are long distances to travel by compass, and changes in direction are necessary at places where there are no identifying features, but the procedure is the same. On the return, set the compass out, let the needle stop swinging, and set north on the dial to the north end of the needle. Walk in the direction your notes indicate, trying to keep on the proper heading, and you should arrive at the next known point without difficulty.

This knowledge is a real safeguard in high open country above timberline. Frequently the snow is so firm that no real snowshoe tracks are left. If clouds move in, and a little snow blows into what tracks there are, a whiteout occurs. The effect can be so complete it is hard to tell where the surface is until your snowshoe actually touches it. A whiteout can be very confusing, even on a small open area, but if you can travel from known point to known point by compass you are well prepared for the task. The same problem exists in gentle, low-elevation country. Crossing large frozen lakes in poor visibility requires a compass.

The most difficult route finding is in featureless, rolling country such as the foothills on the fringes of mountain ranges. In gentle country you can be on or near a

BIGfoot says ▶▶
A hike you've done in the summer will take longer on snowshoes, and daylight hours are much shorter, so turnaround times need to be sooner.

divide and cross into another stream valley without realizing it, then follow it down away from the starting point.

The compass is of little help unless you are at a known point and want to get to another known point. To find your way cross-country without a trail, where there are no visible landmarks, you must prepare information such as compass bearings on the way in to have the accurate information necessary to get out in a storm.

Another method of checking distance traveled is to use your **watch** for **elapsed time** and **estimated speed.** At a speed of 2 mph, it will take thirty minutes to go 1 mile. Faster or slower speeds can be figured from this easily remembered number.

Another useful tool for route finding in mountainous terrain is an **altimeter.** Like the compass, it is of little help if you have absolutely no clue as to where you are—visually or on the map. If you have plotted a course on the map and question just where another trail turns off the main trail (because it will probably be covered in snow or could be a little-used trail), use the topo map to note that point in elevation and record it. On that section of trail, the altimeter reading can indicate that this must be the spot to make the turn. Because altimeters are based on barometer pressure, weather changes affect their accuracy. The initial reading must be set for the actual elevation at the start of your trek, then corrected every hour or so to the elevation of known points along the route that will be recognizable from the topo map. If obvious changes are happening in the weather, corrections will need to be done more often to be accurate. Studying the maps of the area is the best preparation for accurate route finding.

If all else fails, the **Global Positioning System (GPS)** can help you find your position and point you on your way through a system of triangulation. With a minimum of three satellites signaling to a small, handheld GPS receiver, your position can be displayed on the screen in the form of either latitude/longitude or Universal Transverse Mercator (UTM) coordinates, or even as a map location. Add at least a fourth satellite and you may know the altitude. The GPS can be preprogramed with your intended route, with preset positions recorded along the way, to help you get there and back. Additional information displayed on most units can include distance traveled, rate of travel, and estimated time to destination. The GPS receiver must have a direct "line-of-sight" to

> **BIGfoot says ▶▶**
> If your altimeter is a part of a GPS system using more than three satellites, altitude accuracy will not be affected by barometric pressure.

enough satellites to calculate your position without being obstructed by thick tree cover, down in a deep valley, or in a narrow canyon. Always carry extra batteries since they deplete faster in winter temperatures. Keeping the GPS receiver in a warm place next to your body and turning it off when not in use will help to preserve the batteries. Consider these units a complement to the map and compass, not a replacement. And, practice is necessary to become efficient enough to keep from getting confused and lost.

Snowshoers are getting farther into the mountains each winter. In addition to the increased avalanche danger from heavy snowfall in steep country, a new challenge is being accepted in winter: glacier travel. Route finding is the same on a glacier, winter or summer. Note the crevasses, some of which remain open all winter, and pick a route around them, as you would in summer. The hollows are usually safer because the glacier surface is under compression and crevasses seldom occur there. Areas where the surface is shoved up, such as a large mound a quarter-mile or so across, generally are heavily crevassed, since the surface is under tension.

In winter there is much less indication of crevasses than in summer, when there is no snowfall and warm temperatures cause faster glacier movement. Unless the distance and depth are very great, windblown snow may bridge even wide crevasses by the same process that builds snow cornices out 10 to 20 feet on the lee side of ridges. When the cornice does bridge the crevasse, the snow drifts across and leaves no clue that a few feet down is unsupported snow. It is doubtful that any but small crevasses fill completely with windblown snow, and many holes lie under the apparently innocent, smooth glacier in winter and summer. One additional problem in winter is that it is difficult to locate crevasses by probing with an ice ax. The snow is so soft every-where that plunging the shaft in to the head does not necessarily indicate a crevasse underneath.

Snowshoes decrease the chance of stepping through a weak snow bridge by distributing the weight over a large area. It is likely that only a very wide, weak bridge would collapse under a person wearing footgear 3 feet long. However, in winter as in summer, keep the party roped up.

Crevasse rescue on snowshoes is the same as with crampons, except that the person being rescued places the boot heel, rather than the toe, in the slings (unless one can remove snowshoes while hanging from the climbing rope without losing

them down the crevasse). As in summer, ice axes must be used for belays (the ice-ax basket must be removed to belay, so be sure it is quickly detachable). Raising techniques are described in *Mountaineering: The Freedom of the Hills* (see Suggested Reading). Study the techniques before going into crevassed terrain.

Cold temperatures slow the movement of glaciers. However, icefalls are active all winter, so choose your route, as you would in summer, to minimize dangers of seracs falling on the climbing party. It is surprising how many blocks tumble down icefalls at night in zero temperature. But major activity is in the morning, after sunlight hits the ice and warms it even slightly; after sundown, when the chill begins to freeze the ice a little harder; and anytime in between.

In summary, there are several things for beginning snowshoers to remember. First, be familiar with the area you are in. Second, follow a trail if possible. Third, when the trail is obscured by snow, pick a route that avoids dangers and obstructions and is guided by prominent landmarks. Fourth, mark the return trail with flags or wands in case it storms and landmarks are not visible for the return; and carry a map and compass and correlate them with your route. Fifth, have a plan for survival if you must stay overnight or longer and wait out a storm.

These rules are not fun and games—there simply isn't enough dumb luck to supply all who need it.

CHAPTER 11

Winter Safety

Many objective hazards of winter travel cannot be predicted with any great degree of accuracy; instead, they must be observed and evaluated. It is possible to say a particular slope is prone to avalanche, or that large globs of snow fall off trees after heavy storms, but on-the-spot judgments of the immediate danger must be made in each particular case. The hazards described here should convince you of the necessity of both learning about the dangers in the winter backcountry and of leaving a detailed itinerary with friends before your trip.

LAKES AND STREAMS

Snow travelers occasionally fall through the ice covering a stream or lake. Lakes may

◀◀ ▲ *New snow is one sign of potential avalanche hazards.*

have 2 or 3 feet of ice on them and still have some hazards. The main one, aside from insufficient ice to walk on safely, is a spring entering a lake. The relatively warmer spring water will melt the ice or prevent the spot from freezing, which causes a weak spot. Note places along the margin of the lake where snow depth is less. These may indicate such a spring.

Snowshoers crossing lakes that have many inches of ice sometimes wade into slush on top of the ice, even on subzero days. This may be water from a stream that has frozen at the shore but continues to seep a small amount of water on top of the ice under an insulating layer of snow. This does not necessarily indicate weak and dangerous ice.

Some people believe that a great weight of snow on a solidly frozen lake will crack the ice and permit water to well up, causing a weak area that is better avoided. (In the Cascade Range of the Pacific Northwest there may be no ice on a lake; what appears to be a lake with thick ice and a snow cover is in reality several feet of snow floating on the lake with no ice at all.)

Generally mountain streams flow too fast to freeze into good access routes. The main problem is that they are open and deep all winter. Eight to ten feet of snow on either bank makes them as formidable as a crevasse in a glacier. If there is no bridge or footlog, the hike may necessarily end at the stream crossing. Even when there is a bridge, it may be dangerous to cross. Walking on a narrow ridge of snow

8 feet above the bridge decking and even farther above the streambed calls for flawless technique: sidestep across very gently, keeping the feet directly over the bridge. If you are using a footlog, it may be safer to clear the snow off, although this may expose frozen and icy bark. Sidestepping may leave snowshoe tails and toes hanging out in the air if the log is narrow, a frightening view for some.

Instep crampons on modern snowshoes provide the greatest security on slippery footlogs and icy stones in streams, biting into these surfaces much better than any rubber-soled boot. If the water is deep, unhook one shoulder strap and the waist-band of your pack to make it easier to jettison in case you fall into the water. If a rope is available, it is a good idea to rope up or rig a hand line for safety on dangerous stream crossings. It may not be possible to stop someone from landing in the creek, but the rope will ensure he or she gets out.

Where there is no log or bridge, or where one is impassable, it may be possible to dig a trail down the snow wall on one side of the stream, step across, and dig a ramp up the wall on the other side. Be careful to keep your snowshoes out of the water if traveling in powder snow; several pounds of powder will freeze on wet snowshoes in the first steps, unless they happen to be plastic. Use extreme caution when crossing streams that are frozen over or bridged with snow, especially if the water underneath is deeper than your boot tops.

Use all necessary precautions to avoid getting in water. Other party members should be ready with ice axes, rope, or handy poles to provide firmly anchored handholds to help any unfortunate snowshoer back out if the ice breaks. It's hard to pull your snowshoes out of a mass of slush and ice chunks, and also very unpleasant to reach bare hands down in the frigid mass to unbuckle bindings to make a less encumbered exit from the icy stream—and way too dangerous!

IDIOT MAKERS

Part of the attraction of winter is walking among snow-covered trees—they can be even more lovely than in summer. At times they are covered so deeply that no green shows, and the top or a high branch may have an accumulation of snow weighing many pounds. Periodically these huge

BIGfoot says ▶▶

CAUTION! Do not step in water while snowshoeing. Water on equipment, clothing, or your body freezes. Use your poles to probe for wet conditions.

bombs—called idiot makers where I come from—fall out of trees a hundred or more feet tall, landing with a "whoomp," and making an impact crater in the snow. I know of no one who has been injured by one, but from personal experience, I know they can knock you flat and make you very wet. Keep a wary eye open when the trees are carrying heavy loads of snow in their tops; wearing a hard hat isn't too bad an idea in this situation.

These treetop snow globs are a phenomenon of heavy snow country, where snow falls softly and silently without wind. At higher elevations, especially on ridge tops, trees appear to be completely covered with snow. This is usually rime ice, which is formed when wind-driven mist freezes on trees or rocks upon contact. (A tap with your hand will indicate that the rime is anything but soft.)

WHITEOUTS

In dense fog, clouds, and often blowing snow there may be no visual clues to location. Sky and snow merge, the horizon disappears, and it is difficult to tell whether you are walking uphill or downhill. Until you touch it with an ice ax, pole, or snowshoe, it is impossible to tell where the surface is. Frequently people walk off drifts and tumble down because they simply cannot see the drop-off, and all the victims' companions know is that they have somehow disappeared. The only way to move in a whiteout is very carefully, even roped up to each other. It can be the ultimate test of your route-finding skills.

The whiteouts—actually snowstorms— that affect the most people are probably the ones above tree line in New York's Adirondacks, New Hampshire's White Mountains, and Maine's Mount Katahdin. The various mountain and hiking clubs there have gone to great effort to mark the trails to help hikers and climbers find their way off high places in the frequent times of limited visibility. Rock cairns several feet high and closely spaced mark many of the trails on the Presidential Range and Franconia Ridge, the two highest and most heavily used ridges in White Mountain National Forest. The people who climb these mountains in winter in "normal" conditions of subzero temperatures and 30-mph wind are just plain tough. There's no place else where people get out of the car when weather conditions are that hostile.

BIGfoot says ▶▶
What a whiteout looks like in the wild:

The tempting thing about climbing these relatively low-elevation peaks is that there is not a great distance from tree line to the summits, except in the Presidential Range, where the elevation rises to 1,800 feet. Most of these peaks are very accessible, generally one-day climbs, and the danger of avalanches is mainly in sheltered areas on the lee side. On higher mountains where there is a vast area above timberline, such as the 8,000 feet or so of elevation from forest to summit on Washington's Mount Rainier, it is less tempting to tough it out in a storm, and impossible to make a summit climb.

ABOVE TREE LINE

This section was added to the third edition (and retained in the fourth and fifth) mainly due to the May 1986 accident on Mount Hood in Oregon. A group of teenagers with adult leaders attempted a summit climb of the 11,245-foot mountain. A storm developed, with high winds, subfreezing temperatures, and blizzard conditions. The decision to turn back was made after some members of the party were too tired and cold to get off the mountain.

The hikers dug a snow cave, where the weaker ones stayed while the two strongest traveled to a road, where help was summoned. The storm continued for several days, which prevented an effective search. By the time the cave was located, only two of the nine who took shelter could be revived.

Many people have run afoul of storms above tree line in spring, summer, and fall in the mountains of the United States. One such site is in the Washington Cascades at Goat Rocks, where the Pacific Crest Trail goes over Old Snowy Mountain, an elevation of 7,930 feet and well above tree line. One fatality and several near-fatalities occurred here when a summer-equipped party encountered winter temperatures and blizzard conditions.

These unpredictable winter-strength storms can be expected from Labor Day (and before) through autumn and into June the next year. In the eastern mountains, the ferocity and frequency of storms is of such impact that hiking and climbing clubs and the U.S. Forest Service and other public officials make a great effort to inform the public of the danger. In August 1986, a snowstorm in the Presidential Range led to one death due to hypothermia on Mount Madison.

Death is a fact in every U.S. mountain range, as marked by place names like Cadaver Gap on Mount Rainier and Froze to Death Plateau in the Beartooths of Montana, just two of a long list. Storm-caused fatalities are a significant part of the total mountain death toll.

BIGfoot says ▶▶
Besides unpredictable high winds, subfreezing temperatures, and blizzard conditions, the abilities of everyone in your group must be taken into consideration. The trip must be geared to the "weakest" or least prepared person.

Like the many drowning victims who never intended to enter the water, a large percentage of people who died in mountain storms never intended to get into a snowstorm with subfreezing temperatures and severe wind chill. They didn't realize what they had committed themselves to until it was too late to get down the mountain or back out of the storm.

Be aware that encountering storms above tree line exposes you to a far greater risk than does finding yourself in a storm on a forest trail. Include winter clothing in your pack when the trip involves going above tree line. When caught in such a storm, either get the tent up quickly, before your party is too weak and chilled to do so, or turn back while your party has the strength to move into sheltering forest.

AVALANCHES

By far the most spectacular hazard in winter is a snow avalanche. Large avalanche chutes descending through heavy forest from ridge-top snowfields are easy to recognize and avoid. Small slides are a greater hazard than huge ones because there are more of them and they aren't as obviously powerful and destructive. Man is totally outmatched when caught in sliding snow; a layer only 6 inches deep and 20 feet wide sliding less than 100 feet can bury a person.

Big avalanches involve tremendous tonnages of snow and develop a great deal of momentum. Besides ripping out trees on the edge of their paths and in the areas where they stop, they can run up opposite slopes. Some travel long distances on level ground after a rapid descent. With enough speed, a moving snow mass can climb up hillsides where a containing gully makes sharp turns. When snow drops over a cliff in a gully there is a roar like thunder. Nature on the rampage, as these avalanches testify, is an awesome thing.

AVALANCHE CONDITIONS

There are four main conditions causing snow to slide off mountains. **First,** during a storm the snow builds to a depth and weight that exceeds its ability to adhere to the snow or rock surface beneath, so it slides. The majority of avalanches occur during and immediately after storms. **Second,** wind picks up snow on the windward side of ridges and deposits it on the lee side, or in any sheltered place. This layer may slide during or soon after the storm as a loose, unconsolidated mass. Or, it may settle into a firm mass, and over the course of days or weeks the bond between it and the surface below may weaken until the entire layer slides as a slab. It is not necessary for snow to drift anywhere to form slab. The fact that snow falls when the wind is blowing is sufficient to cause it to form a wind slab that may slide soon after the snow is deposited or remain unstable days or weeks later. The **third** condition is a rising temperature that melts newly fallen snow. The mass is lubricated by the moisture, and the bond with the underlying snow deteriorates until either the upper layer or the whole mass slides. The **fourth** is depth hoar. The formation of these hoar frost crystals at depth in the snowpack weakens the bond between two layers of snow.

One important factor that has a bearing on avalanches, usually of the slab type, is depth hoar. This is a zone or layer of distinctive cup- or needle-shaped crystals, caused by water vapor either from the ground or from the snowpack's lower layers rising and refreezing within it. Vapor rises through the snowpack all winter long. It may freeze on the surface at about 0°F and look like frost "feathers," called *surface hoar.*

If the temperature drops well below zero the upper part of the snowpack is chilled to air temperature and water vapor freezes at some depth rather than on the surface— thus the term *depth hoar.* These crystals do not bond together and therefore form a weak layer within the snowpack that acts like an air space. On steep slopes anything that breaks the overlying layer of snow causes a slide as the depth hoar layer helps weaken or destroy the bond with the snow below. There is a "whoomp" as the upper layers collapse and settle.

Depth hoar is most likely to form in any weak layers or crust within the snowpack. These conditions have been noted under ice layers in the East. Because water vapor cannot rise through this barrier, depth hoar forms, which snowshoers discover as the upper layers settle. The longer the severe subzero temperature persists, the deeper the snowpack is chilled, so depth hoar may form right on the ground. For example, one February a group of us started a climbing trip in the Purcell Range in British Columbia. Several weeks of –20° to –30°F temperatures had created a depth hoar layer through the Rockies and other mountain ranges in Canada. Pits we dug in the 4-foot-deep snowpack showed that the bottom 15 to 18 inches was depth hoar. A snow cave in a 9-foot-deep drift at 7,200 feet showed the same. Mountaineering was out of the question, so we substituted a route protected by dense forest to Lake of the Hanging Glacier. Everywhere we went the slab settled under us.

Cracks radiated out from us on the level logging road approach. Cracks appeared under the trailbreaker's snowshoes, and every 50 yards or so the "whoomp" of settling slab jarred our nerves. Cracks appeared on the edges of the trail and around trees, and small bushes shook, but after several days the sound almost lost its shock value as we nearly became accustomed to it. During our stay, more and more slab avalanche fracture lines appeared on slopes of the 10,000- to 11,000-foot peaks high above our forest-protected route.

The most valuable information we received on avoiding trouble was from our guide, Arnor Larson, who has climbed for years in winter in the Purcells and is knowledgeable about avalanche hazards there. Depth hoar is not supposed to be a hazard on glaciers. It is doubtful that water vapor would rise hundreds of feet through glacial ice and refreeze as hoar beneath the surface snowpack. However, at the time of our outing, over the previous two months ten skiers had lost their lives in depth hoar–associated slab avalanches in British Columbia alone. Our party decided to stay off steep glaciers that looked like superb avalanche terrain and let someone else field-test the validity of whether there is depth hoar on glaciers.

When a layer of snow is unstable, anything that disturbs it can trigger a slide—a snowshoer, a skier, snow falling out of a tree or from a cliff above. Avalanche-control methods in ski areas and on highways include explosives to trigger the snow into sliding or to stabilize it further when it will not slide.

Avalanches follow gullies off the sides of ridges and down mountain faces. These may be spotted easily where there is forest cover. Lee slopes below cornices are common areas of wind slab. Snow cornices indicate a lot of windblown snow on the side they overhang. Forest cover isn't foolproof, as snow can slide through fairly closely spaced trees like water, inflicting additional injuries as the victim ricochets off trees. Only if the trees are "as thick as the hair on a dog's back," to quote one U.S. Forest Service ranger, can you be sure it will not slide. In one instance, a slide filtered a skier through very closely set trees, stripping him of skis, poles, hat, glasses, and mitts and inflicting severe injuries.

Powder snow avalanches generally occur at high elevations where temperatures remain cold. Much powder snow sloughs off the steepest slopes during storms; it is most dangerous where wind has deposited piles of it in sheltered gullies. The speed of the sliding snow is great, and the air pushed ahead of the avalanche results in a preceding wind blast that is as destructive as the snow itself. The powder snow menace is not usually as severe on the volcanic peaks of the Cascades, possibly because they are quite rounded and have few high sheltering ridges where it can collect. On these open slopes the wind packs the snow as it falls. However, there are places on Mount Rainier where windblown snow accumulates and creates avalanche danger. Between 11,000 and 12,000 feet the Ingraham Glacier, in the lee of Gibraltar Rock, catches enough snow to plug, or at least cover, its many huge crevasses each winter. At another point just under 7,000 feet, Panorama Point faces into the prevailing southwest wind. Here it forms both slab and powder avalanches that have killed a few of the many people who have snowshoed, skied, and hiked up it toward 10,000-foot Camp Muir. When a pile of windblown snow on a lee slope congeals into a somewhat solid mass, it is called a slab. As it settles, the slab adheres to itself and tends to shrink, and the process weakens the bond with the underlying layer. The joint between the two layers may develop depth hoar during a spell of –20° F or so temperatures. This zone is less dense than either the slab above or the slab below, and the area sounds hollow underfoot. As the bond weakens, it eventually reaches a point at which the slightest jar can trigger a slide.

When it slides, the slab, several inches to several feet in depth, breaks off from stable snow in a vertical fracture that may run for several hundred feet. The sliding mass may start over a large area and break into many blocks. The danger in a slab avalanche is that many tons of snow may remain poised for weeks and then be released all at once. Apparently not as sensitive to rising temperature as powder snow, many slabs are triggered in the Cascades in April and May when overhanging cornices crash onto the snow below. Of course, cornices themselves, which may form on both sides of a ridge within a short distance, are a hazard to anyone below, whether they trigger any further avalanche or not.

Slab is formed by conditions of heavy snowfall and high winds in mountains and hills, and even on flats. These slabs on flat areas also sound hollow and sometimes settle a little with a "whoomp." If the snow on the flats is settling as you snowshoe over it, there will be slab formations on the ridges too. And if the road cuts have slab avalanches spontaneously released on them, the high country is no place to be. Normally the deeper your web sinks, the

BIGfoot says ▶▶
Snowpack reacts like elastic when forces such as gravity pull against it. Like a rubber band, it then snaps and releases an avalanche. If a snowshoer moves quickly on the snowpack, or if it is very brittle, it breaks immediately.

firmer the snow becomes, but occasionally your snowshoe settles through the snow, which seems to be hollow, or softer, underneath. This may be an indication that you should not venture out on steep, high mountain slopes for a few days until the snow has stabilized.

AVALANCHE DETECTION

The only sure way to check for slab avalanche hazard is to dig a pit and make a simple test (Figure 31). This involves carrying a shovel, which should be a requirement for outings in avalanche terrain. Choice of a spot to dig requires some thought. It should be in a spot that will not avalanche, but in snow of the same structure and exposure as the slope that is of concern.

Probably at the side of the slope, but within the forest or some other protection, is the safest spot. Dig the pit all the way to the ground to check it out thoroughly. Areas with slab avalanche hazard don't usually have 10 to 15 feet of snow, so the job is not as formidable as it sounds.

Leave a protruding section on the uphill side of the pit, as in Figure 31. Cut a smooth wall and run a finger down it to note hard layers. Check visually for snow crystals that indicate depth hoar. Needle- and cup-shaped crystals do not consolidate and thus indicate a hazard. Use a dark-colored mitten for background and possibly a small magnifying glass to check thoroughly.

The final check is with the shovel. Cut down through the snow on the protruding section of wall, as illustrated. If the layers of snow slide off, there is danger of an avalanche, so don't proceed out on the slope with this hazardous snow on it.

Anyone can recognize the danger in big avalanche slopes and gullies. The hard part is to act on what you know when in the gray area of possible hazard on a small, moderately steep, open slope.

Different mountain regions of the country have different avalanche hazards, which depend on weather conditions. A brief survey is in order.

Pacific Northwest: Wet snow avalanches are the most predictable type and are most typical of the wet, warm Pacific Northwest. The textbook sequence of events leading to release of these heavy, relatively slow-moving slides is as follows: cold, moist air from the Pacific Ocean moves across the Cascades, dropping several feet of snow. This air mass is pushed out by a warmer one; the snow is warmed to melting, becomes wet, and settles. Weight increases as it picks up water from the warm, moist air. The bond between the new snow and the underlying layer becomes lubricated and the mass slides. Wet snow a few inches to several feet in depth can slide. Weight is very great although speed is slow compared to powder snow. Wet snow rolls into balls,

BIGfoot says ▸▸

Even after you know what the books and the experts say, you must use creative common sense and stay away from even gray areas of possible danger.

Figure 31. Checking for slab avalanche hazard

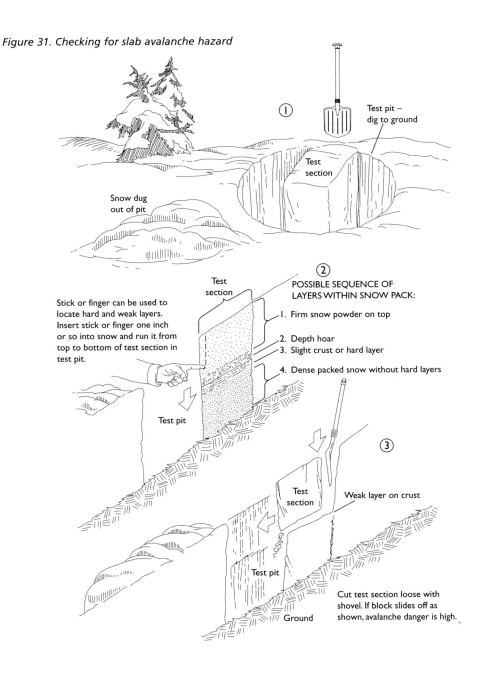

① Test pit –
dig to ground

Test section

Snow dug out of pit

② POSSIBLE SEQUENCE OF LAYERS WITHIN SNOW PACK:

Test section

Stick or finger can be used to locate hard and weak layers. Insert stick or finger one inch or so into snow and run it from top to bottom of test section in test pit.

1. Firm snow powder on top

2. Depth hoar

3. Slight crust or hard layer

4. Dense packed snow without hard layers

Test pit

③

Test section

Weak layer on crust

Test pit

Cut test section loose with shovel. If block slides off as shown, avalanche danger is high.

Ground

Photos by BIGfoot Snowshoe Tours

This area slides often enough to have a name, "The Professor." It is located across from Arapahoe Basin Ski Area in the Colorado Rockies.

(Top) "The Professor" without snow (Bottom) One avalanche chute of the "Seven Sisters" near Loveland Pass Road in the Colorado Rocky Mountains

ranging from a few inches in size to several feet across. It normally freezes to ice when it stops.

I've helped dig a lot of holes and snow caves in Cascade snow, but never found out anything about depth hoar. For example, the subzero temperatures necessary to create depth hoar are not as common in this relatively warm area. So it is probably more valuable for an individual to learn to recognize where avalanches occur than to understand exactly why the snow cuts loose and swoops down mountainsides.

There are also powder snow and wind slab avalanches in the Cascades. Winter avalanche hazard may begin as early as October and does not end until May, June, or July, depending on late-season storms.

Eastern Mountains: Here the greatest hazard from avalanches occurs on the lee sides of the Presidential Range and Mount Katahdin; they usually are the wind slab variety. Depth hoar can be a factor, as temperatures frequently drop well below zero. There is also the possibility of ice layers from January thaws, which have an effect on depth hoar formation as well as forming a good base for avalanches.

The areas of greatest hazard are the exposed lee slopes above tree line, and the slides, treeless chutes descending from mountaintops to forest.

In New Hampshire, Tuckerman and Huntington Ravine headwalls are heavily climbed and skied once they are snow-covered. These steep glacial cirques avalanche often after each snowfall, and avalanche warnings are posted daily at Pinkham Notch. Avalanches also endanger the steep headwalls and slides in less traveled Great Gulf, King Ravine, and above tree line on Franconia Ridge in New Hampshire and on Mount Katahdin in Maine, to mention only a few.

Wet snowslides occur as temperatures warm in spring; these are not as much snowshoeing hazards as they are spring mountaineering dangers.

Rocky Mountains: It is hard to generalize about an area as large as the Rockies and the associated ranges of Wyoming, Montana, Colorado, New Mexico, Arizona, Idaho, British Columbia, and Alberta. Normally, the subzero cold of December and January causes depth hoar formation. Subsequent snowfalls insulate it, and it may persist into February and March or later. The result is a serious avalanche hazard on slopes; later, snowfall with wind and resultant wind slab and slab formed from snowfall without wind may increase the hazard.

Only by checking in the field can the degree of danger be determined. Snow may firm by March, making good traveling.

Warm days in late winter and spring consolidate the snow and depth hoar, but on north slopes the hazard persists longer. The local climbers get avalanched frequently enough to give ample warning about the danger that depth hoar and wind slab create. It is sensible to use information from every agency and authority when planning a mountain trip in these areas. Fortunately, there are untouched areas for touring and hiking that are not as menaced by slides. Every winter Yellowstone National Park plays host to more people on touring skis.

Colorado and the mountains to the north have some similar avalanche hazards. Subzero temperatures form depth hoar, which creates severe hazard. Subsequent snowfall, as in all other depth hoar areas, insulates the hoar zone deep within the snowpack, preserving it until warmer late-winter or spring temperatures consolidate it.

Sometimes by February deep, soft snow has firmed up and traveling is easier. Snow above timberline may be stable earlier, as wind and sun firm it sooner than on shaded slopes and under trees in the forested areas. By early April there is often a lot of sun, which may warm the snowpack to form a crust on which snowshoers can bare-boot it. In comparison to the Cascades, there is a lot of sun all winter long.

Some years, March and April see heavy snowfall with wind and resultant wind slab. Again, avalanche warnings for highways and ski areas give valuable information to the snow traveler. Before starting out on a mountain trip, people unfamiliar with the area should use U.S. Forest Service snow and avalanche reports and locate a local authority or knowledgeable person. Generalizations are helpful, but only a field check on snow formation in the area you intend to use will provide valid avalanche hazard information.

When avalanche hazard is high, pick hikes and climbs free of danger. These will be in the lower, gentler hills, which are a part of the extensive and complex ranges of Colorado. Colorado has the highest number of reported avalanches of any state, and yearly death totals could be greatly reduced with more caution by mountain travelers. The Colorado Avalanche Information Center, based in Denver, provides up-to-date avalanche forecasts from November through April. Phone numbers are listed for most of the primary regions throughout the state: Denver/Boulder, (303) 275-5360; Fort Collins, (970) 482-0457; Colorado Springs, (719) 520-0020; Durango, (970) 247-8187; Summit County, (970) 668-0600; and U.S. Forest Service/Aspen, (970) 920-1664, and Vail, (970) 479-4652.

Wasatch: The same general weather pattern as the Rockies occurs in the Wasatch Range in Utah. Deep powder snow is to be expected in December and January, with spells of severe subzero temperatures that cause the formation of depth hoar. Snow usually falls with the wind, causing wind slab, especially in the high mountains. Movies at the U.S. Forest Service Avalanche Study Center near Alta, Utah, testify to the danger of slab avalanches, whether influenced by wind slab or depth hoar.

Deep snow over the depth hoar layer may cause it to persist throughout the winter, as in other mountain areas described already. South slopes firm up earliest, but south slopes warmed by the sun in late winter present the greatest spring avalanche hazard, generally of the wet snow type.

Winter may begin in October, and powder snow can still be expected at higher elevations through April and May. Heavy storms may occur any month, as the storm patterns within each area are capricious. Once more, use all available avalanche warning information. There are avalanche-free routes on gentler terrain and smaller peaks north of the main Wasatch.

Sierra Nevada: These mountains also have severe early winter subzero weather with its resultant depth hoar formation. The depth hoar layer often lasts through the winter as subsequent snowfalls cover it, insulating the weak zone from warmth that tends to stabilize the snowpack. Normal snowfall is several feet deep, although there are drought years when snowfall is light. Winter can begin in late September and October, but late November and December is more usual. Deep powder with danger of wind slab is usual in December, January, and February. The weather pattern in this vast mountain area is as changeable as each of the other winter areas discussed. March, April, and even May can be months of greatest snowfall.

Spring slab avalanches can be due to depth hoar formed in early winter. Often by February snow is firm enough for good snow travel in the foothills east of the main Sierra and the Southern California peaks. By March and April the snow on the high peaks and valleys may firm up. This depends entirely on the weather pattern for the year, and avalanche danger and travel conditions must be evaluated on the spot. Ski area and highway avalanche warnings are a real help, as in the other areas where people snowshoe and tour.

AVALANCHE SURVIVAL

There is much discussion among snowshoers of what to do when caught in an avalanche. If you can still think and react to the situation it seems best to get on your back, try to stay on top of the sliding snow making swimming motions with your legs and arms, and attempt to move to one side. Try to position your arms to keep a breathing space in front of your face. If you are standing and the snow you are on begins to slide, sit facing downhill.

Regard your efforts as a fight for your life and do everything possible to achieve that end. If your hand, foot, or clothing or attached equipment is visible on the surface, your companions are very likely to recover you alive. Your evasive action may keep you from getting buried, or you may crawl out of a partial burial on your own. A victim found in less than fifteen minutes, especially if buried less than 1 foot deep, will have an 80 percent chance of surviving. At 30 minutes and 2 feet deep, the chances are less than 50 percent for survival. The longer the time and deeper the burial, the grimmer the survival statistics.

Remember that after a person is found, there will probably be some digging, and avalanche snow is often very dense and packed hard when the slide stops. Have more than one shovel in your party in case one shovel is buried with the victim.

The best cure is prevention: the best prevention if there is no way around an avalanche hazard is to end the outing. Next best would be to cross narrow chutes one person at a time with lookouts posted to warn of an approaching slide. If the day is becoming very warm and there is deep new snow with no recent avalanches around, get to a protected place. Wet snowslides are more frequent on warm afternoons than on crisp cold mornings. Some persons who are exposed to avalanches use avalanche cord, dark-colored nylon cord about an eighth of an inch in diameter and up to 100 feet long. One end is tied to the waist and the rest is dragged when crossing a particularly dangerous area. Should a person be caught in a slide, there is a good chance that part of the cord will show, telling rescuers where to start digging. More modern devices are discussed below.

Experience in mountaineering, snowshoeing, and skiing increase your chances of getting caught in an avalanche. A limited study showed sixty-nine avalanche fatalities were people with advanced skills, thirteen were intermediates, and eleven were novices. Chances are it took highly skilled people to get far enough from the car in winter to enter avalanche country. The beginners just may not have been tough enough to get to where they could get killed!

Restraint in avoiding high avalanche hazard comes hard to the male of the species. A study of avalanche deaths in the United States from 1950 to 1987 by Betsy R. Armstrong, showed that 88 percent of these deaths were men, the highest concentration being in the twenty- to twenty-nine-year-old age group. It would appear that to try to warn people—especially males—of the possibility of getting killed while enjoying winter recreation in a beautiful mountain setting is about as effective as warning people about AIDS; a few, by their actions, deny that anything that much fun in such an attractive setting could have a hidden hazard.

Actually, no one seems to have very satisfactory evasive tactics or survival secrets. My own experience in two avalanches was that it was over so quickly there wasn't time to do very much. Both times I turned and faced downhill. In a few seconds my feet worked through the sliding snow and caught in the layer underneath, then the sliding snow behind pitched me forward on hands and knees. This is not the way to ride an avalanche because my head could have hit any obstruction first and the powder eddying around my face made breathing difficult. Once at the mercy of the avalanche, I no longer had any choice in matters of direction and position.

Avalanche victim detectors—small radio transceivers that transmit a radio signal that can be received by a similar unit—are

> **BIGfoot says ▶▶**
> Avalanche snow sets up like concrete. Buying an avalanche shovel is no time to worry about price. Ask questions at the shop about shovel and handle strength and buy the best to save a life.

available. The unit on a buried victim transmits a signal, speeding location of the person—provided there is another unit to receive that signal on a person not buried.

For the detector to be of value, all members of a party must have one and they must wear it, not store it in a pack, which can be swept away in an avalanche. The batteries should be fresh at the start, then kept warm (next to your body), and checked before entering avalanche country. During regular activities, the transceiver's three-way switch (transmit-receive-off) must be set to transmit.

Tracking the detector's signal takes training and a lot of practice to be useful in case of an unexpected emergency (check with your local outdoor store for available clinics and instruction). Try locating a buried transceiver. With your detector set to receive and earpiece firmly set in your ear, walk around until you pick up the signal or beep. The closer you are, the louder the beep. Mark the location and continue beyond it to determine that the signal gets weaker. Sometimes there will be a second place with a strong signal, but this is something like a "skip" in short-wave radio and is actually some yards from the buried instrument.

Return to the marked place, and move away in several directions to get the best location. The area of strongest signal isn't always pinpointed to a square-foot area but may be a circle 8 to 10 feet across. Practice will increase your skill so you don't have to dig a room-sized area.

In areas of managed avalanche control, a snowshoer can run an additional risk. Explosive artillery shells are fired at ridges above roads and human habitation to trigger small slides before the snow becomes deep enough to cause a really damaging avalanche. Be sure to check with local authorities before entering areas subject to such control.

There is no accurate way of predicting the hour, day, or week of most slides. The longer the exposure to danger, the greater the likelihood of getting caught. The best you can do is to recognize that deep, uncon-solidated snow on open slopes and gullies is likely to slide soon after a storm. Be wary of fairly gentle slopes of 20 degrees or more; these may lure people onto them because they don't look as hazardous as 45 degrees or steeper. Warming weather after a heavy snowfall will quickly cause avalanches. Lee slopes are very likely to avalanche after heavy snowfall accompanied by high winds, and the danger remains for weeks after the storm.

Obviously the only 100 percent sure way to avoid getting caught in an avalanche is not to be in a place where there might be one. There is seldom any totally safe time in the mountains during winter and into early spring. The higher elevations do not firm up as soon as lower slopes. Cornices fall off ridge tops until June or later.

The conditions I prefer for a trip in the Cascades into an area of avalanche hazard are several days of warm, clear weather following a storm, then clear, cold, stable weather. The warm weather should flush off the avalanches, and cold temperatures will stabilize the snow.

Each range has its weather pattern. Experienced judgment is the only way to assess the danger, and then it must be based on knowledge of recent weather and the terrain. Use all available information that has a bearing on avalanches: weather and snowfall reports, temperature patterns, mountain pass highway reports, plus avalanche warnings at ski areas and many U.S. national forests. The only choice you have, in the final analysis, is to turn back and not put yourself in an area of potential danger, or continue and accept the risk. But spending the remainder of your life in the few seconds it takes an avalanche to run really doesn't seem to be a truly meaningful snowshoe experience.

AVALANCHE INFORMATION

The study of avalanches is complex and technical. Experts spend their winters

> **BIGfoot says ▶▶**
> I have had two friends die in two separate avalanches. Both were experts! My continuing avalanche education reconsti-tutes my fear enough to stay away from any possible avalanche hazard areas.

collecting data on snowfall, temperatures, and wind velocity, then dig countless pits to observe layers and measure densities. They are gaining much information on why snow slides in avalanches.

Unfortunately, the casual snow traveler may overlook or ignore the data and interpretation of avalanche hazard. Certain areas that are heavily used for winter recreation and main highways that are constantly subject to avalanches do have day-to-day avalanche warnings posted. The U.S. Forest Service has expanded its avalanche warning system in many mountainous areas. Ski areas patrol and check danger zones daily.

There is a great deal of up-to-date information available and snowshoers should take advantage of it. Radio and TV ski reports give a general picture of local or regional snow conditions, so it's best to do some specific research before setting out on a hike or climb in avalanche-prone country. However, most of us who love the solitude of the remote winter backcountry are pretty much on our own.

Three books have been excellent resources for further study: *The Avalanche Handbook* by David McClung and Peter Schaerer; *The ABC of Avalanche Safety* by Edward R. La Chapelle; and *The Avalanche Book* by Betsy R. Armstrong, Knox Williams, and Richard L. Armstrong (see Suggested Reading). Avalanche lectures are a part of most winter outing programs sponsored by hiking and climbing clubs, along with local mountain shops. There are also avalanche schools in many mountain areas. Here are two of the better known:

National Avalanche School
National Ski Patrol System
133 South Van Gordon Street, Suite 100
Lakewood, CO 80228
(303) 988-1111

American Avalanche Institute
Box 308
Wilson, WY 83014
(307) 733-3315

SEARCH AND RESCUE

Over the years people have been lost, injured, or killed in the mountains and backcountry through avalanches, hypothermia, and other hazards, so a chain of responsibility has developed to organize and put into action search and rescue procedures. In Washington, the county sheriffs have been delegated this authority, although certain areas, such as national parks and Indian reservations, have their own organizations, which are independent of state or local control. In New Hampshire, the Department of Fish and Game has this job, and in the national parks of Canada the park wardens are in charge. Although there is no real pattern in the various states, provinces, counties, or towns, rescue responsibility has generally been delegated to an agency or person wherever there is outdoor recreation.

In order for any search and rescue to begin, the information that someone, or a group, has not returned or may be lost has to be reported. Individuals or groups must leave a detailed itinerary with family or friends, with an estimated time of return. Whether rescue depends upon accurate information, a matter of timing, or just plain luck, the life that gets saved may be your own.

The range of problems connected with winter rescues is interesting. The mountain areas of New England are quite compact compared with the many western ranges. The British Columbia director of emergencies has a vast expanse of mountain country and also must be concerned with hunters lost somewhere along logging roads 1,000 miles (1,600 km) long.

As agency personnel changes, so does rescue expertise. There are exceptions, but few sheriffs or game protectors have experienced people with specialized skills on their staff, so in many areas good working arrangements with winter climbers fill this need. Thus much search and rescue work is done by local volunteers under the umbrella of the responsible agency. Most of the burden of evacuation is now borne by helicopters, but there is enough bad weather that grounds aircraft to guarantee that rescuers on foot and on snow machines are still a vital part of the rescue picture. Search dogs trained to locate victims buried in avalanches are in great demand for these emergencies. Well-trained dogs and their owners are flown thousands of miles to smell out victims buried in flood debris as well as in snow.

There is no uniform method of determining how to handle backcountry emergencies. The traditional method of obtaining help is to get word to the local sheriff (or to a ranger if in a national park). In Washington, for example, the sheriff then evaluates the problem and starts organizing the search or rescue. This may involve getting medical aid, calling for volunteers—usually search and rescue and mountain rescue units—to bring the person out, arranging for a helicopter, setting up an air search, bringing in a canine search group, or a combination of methods. State Civil Defense usually helps coordinate efforts, especially if several state and federal agencies are contributing to the operation. Jeep clubs or Explorer Scout search and rescue groups may participate. For large searches, several branches may be involved, using Air Force, Army, and Navy helicopters as well as Civil Air Patrol.

The helicopter has become the real backbone of the backcountry rescue, but the availability of helicopters from MAST (Military Aid for Safety and Traffic) may vary, depending on military involvement elsewhere. Occasionally Coast Guard choppers are also available. Performance has been improved so much since the 1950s that injured climbers have been lifted off Alaska's Mount McKinley at over

17,000 feet, and mountain rescue people have been flown to 14,000 feet on Mount Rainier, then picked up again.

Winter snow closes many access roads and complicates search and rescue. Bad weather is likely to be a factor, too, hampering the use of helicopters and light planes. In fact, just about every wheel- and foot-propelled search group can be stalled on the steps of the sheriff's office. Deep snow isolates the backcountry: a 10-mile round trip in rough country in average snow conditions can be considered a strenuous day on snowshoes. A rescue party on foot needs to carry overnight gear and set up an advance base camp just to get to the backcountry; instead of a quick dash up a trail to the location of the problem, a winter rescue lasts several days to accomplish anything. Obviously people on foot are frequently not able to get to the victim soon enough. Snowmobiles have a good potential for increasing the range of a search party, but most machines move too fast for thorough search and are limited almost entirely to roads in mountain country unless specifically designed for rescue on narrow trails and sled pulling. Foot-powered rescuers may have an aversion to snow machines and few snowmobilers have any experience in searching, let alone snowshoeing. A combination of methods is usually the solution.

For example, in one incident jeeps and snowmobiles were used to transport Tacoma, Washington, mountain rescue people and a German shepherd search group to Corral Pass, north of Mount Rainier, to search for a hunter who had been missing overnight. By getting to the search area quickly and easily, the foot searchers were able to search strenuously and effectively. The hunter was located, and although he was disoriented and somewhat incoherent, he walked out under his own power after being warmed with hot drinks.

Later the same year a similar situation occurred in the east central Washington Cascades. Another hunter was missing in temperatures of about 10° F. The sheriff called in Ellensburg mountain rescue and snowmobile search and rescue personnel, and a search was begun about 11:00 P.M. on snowmobiles. The searchers successfully located the missing man's trail, although it entered country too rugged to follow on machines. It was clear that the victim had to be followed on foot, and two men did so while snowmobiles patrolled roads on the edges of the area. The search was completed when the hunter walked out the next afternoon, with the foot searchers only about half an hour behind him.

As more and more people go out in the hills for winter recreation, it is logical to assume that from time to time they will find themselves in need of outside help. Summer rescue techniques work in winter except for the added problem of snow-covered access roads, which make it difficult to rapidly get to the area where the problem is.

Washington mountain rescue winter training conferences have established that no single rescue organization is adequate to handle a problem 5 to 10 miles from a road in winter. Rescuers on snowshoes and skis are too limited in range to move quickly enough. If they must carry overnight equipment and food for several days, their speed and range are further curtailed. Add to this the general lack of enthusiasm of trained rescue personnel for winter outings under these conditions and the result is a greatly reduced number of people available for such problems. Winter training programs, spending at least one night in a snow camp, have not been well attended. (Personnel for one program received inquiries about the accommodations at the motel convention center nearby.) Winter demands a great deal of searchers, which only experience or winter training sessions can provide.

People who frequent the winter backcountry need to be the basis for improving present backcountry rescue groups. It is good insurance to be an active participant in a functioning group that can get out and help people in trouble in the winter hills. I've limped out after being somewhat mistreated by sliding snow, and a number of other people have had even narrower escapes than that. There is no better motivation than knowing the rescue group you are helping to train may someday come and get you out of trouble.

Again, preparation is invaluable. In case of an accident in your own party in the backcountry, what are you going to do if you need outside help? First, of course, objectively evaluate the situation: don't waste time analyzing the cause. If the problem is an injury, care for the victim and get help. Consider shorter routes out to a road, if any exist. If you need help quickly and there is a good shortcut to a road, go, and later figure out how to get back to your car.

Fortunately, there is an organized volunteer group of rescue people near most winter hiking and climbing areas, whether it's backwoods Canada, New England, or the West. Increased publicity does help to encourage talented winter hikers and climbers to offer their services. Unfortunately, the emphasis sometimes is that a death or injury to a winter hiker is a tragedy and someone should put a stop to this sort of nonsense. My personal philosophy on backcountry accidents is that death and injury are a part of life and occur at home, too, which is supposedly safer.

Do give some thought and time to the subject of winter rescue. If you are asked to participate in such an operation, consider it an honor. Sometimes, in our impersonal and affluent society, one has the impression that no one needs a helping hand. But, if someone is in trouble in the mountains in winter, that person needs help, and may need it desperately.

Through your own search and rescue training and outdoor experience, you become more valuable to yourself or to your group in the event of an emergency. Your best backcountry insurance is training, experience, preparation, and avoiding those situations that will cause need for outside help or rescue.

CHAPTER 12

Tubbs Snowshoe Company

Illness and Injury

Unlike the special safety hazards of winter, the problems discussed in this chapter are, except in unusual circumstances, preventable. Proper equipment, good judgment, and careful attention to early warning signs should make their occurrence as unlikely as some rare tropical disease. There is, however, always a crop of neophytes, or an old-timer who has not learned his lessons well. Any small problem such as a minor injury is intensified by winter conditions; cold is the catalyst that can create real trouble from difficulties you might joke about in summer.

In a typical situation, a party is caught by a storm in a remote area. The first reaction is to continue. Someone becomes tired, so others lend a hand, and they all keep going. Soon it becomes apparent that

◀◀ ▲ *On a safe downhill with avalanche chutes in the background*

they cannot make it out, so they decide to stay overnight. By this time everyone is too wet, cold, and tired to set up good shelter, and because they never intended to camp in a storm, they did not bring the necessary equipment to do so. This can and does happen in summer, but it is obviously more serious in winter.

The combination of fatigue, wet clothing, and cold weather puts too great a strain on an individual with a physical weakness. An undiagnosed minor heart problem or infection in this situation can be fatal. Some people who have become severely chilled may simply die, although others equally miserable survive.

In actual cases in which these conditions have occurred, and in which there have been fatalities, the party has tried to take care of its own problems—the first step in any emergency. But safety is due more to advance preparation than to individual or group heroics during an emergency. If the groups that experienced the fatalities had carried adequate overnight gear the outcome might have been very different.

A lightweight, two-person tent can provide very good bivouac protection. Four people can crowd into it and, seated on foam pads, arrange themselves fairly comfortably. Probably the best way is to sit with two people in one end, facing the other two in the opposite end. This can be done without tent poles or pegs, providing you aren't on a steep snow slope, where you would need to dig a platform. The main problems are that excessive moisture from breath requires ventilation and a resultant heat loss, and that the part of one's body that is tightly pressed against the tent will be cold. Packs or extra clothes might insulate these spots.

A small, lightweight tent thus will shelter four people where a sleeping bag, foam pad, and tarp leave the two or three who can't get in the sleeping bag poorly sheltered. The advantages of sitting facing each other in pairs—or whatever number of people are in the party—is that feet and legs can be overlapped for more comfort than four seated crosswise. Second, cold or frosted toes can be treated easily, and you can watch each other's faces to check on everyone's well-being. A glassy stare might indicate a need for warming. Conversation is easier when facing a person, and some cheering up is sometimes most desirable during the endless hours of a forced winter bivouac.

HYPOTHERMIA

Hypothermia is a more precise name for what is still often referred to as exposure. The problem is that the victim is unable to maintain normal body temperature. When inner body temperature drops below 98.6°F, shivering begins and coordination becomes poor. If chilling continues until body temperature is about 88°F, shivering stops and the victim becomes disoriented and enters a stupor. Unless something is done to stop the loss of body heat and restore normal body temperature, the victim will lose consciousness and die. The air temperature may not be below 50°F, and the victim may have no frostbite or frozen fingertips or toes.

A person who is dehydrated is more subject to chilling and hypothermia than one who is well hydrated. It takes about two quarts of fluid a day to maintain a good fluid balance in your body. Drink enough water so you urinate several times a day. If it stains the snow a deep orange, better drink more water. The concentrated color indicates a lack of water in your system. You lose a surprising amount of water when breathing cold air, not to mention sweating when snowshoeing hard with too many clothes on.

Diagnosing hypothermia is simple; the person is thoroughly chilled, probably very tired, somewhat disoriented, and has poor

BIGfoot says ▶▶
Three good rules for hypothermia prevention, maintaining energy, and general survival are HYDRATE, HYDRATE, HYDRATE. (See more about water containers in Chapter 6, "Other Equipment.")

coordination. Someone who can be warmed will soon be back to normal, but if hypothermia occurs when a party is lost in a snowstorm and has no tent or tarps, the problem is serious. If a tent is available, set it up, strip off wet clothing, and place the victim in a sleeping bag with another person in good condition who can provide body-to-body warmth; or fill canteens with warm—not hot—water and put them in the bag. Hot drinks may suffice if the condition is not serious.

Treatment for hypothermia should be preventive. Be alert to early symptoms and warm chilled people before they become disoriented or enter the advanced stages of hypothermia. The serious hypothermia case develops when there is no easy way to provide shelter. Adequate shelter, hard work, and some real adapting to miserable weather are necessary to warm a badly chilled person in a winter storm or to bring a person already hypothermic at nightfall through the night alive.

It is surprising that a badly hypothermic person, often semiconscious or unconscious, may die in the course of being rescued and warmed. This has mystified rescue personnel.

The explanation was confirmed during postmortem examinations of hypothermia victims, including analysis of their blood. Two factors in particular caused the heart stoppage, and other factors contributed to the death. Warming the victim started blood circulation from the extremities. This blood was still below 98.6°F and very acidic due to the accumulation of impuri-

BIGfoot says ▶▶
Don't overheat to the point of sweating. Wet clothes sap body heat and can freeze!

ties while it was not circulating. The heart, which was already under considerable stress, quit functioning at the added shock of receiving cold, acidic blood.

Understanding this danger has led to a change in the treatment of severely hypothermic people. The unconscious or semiconscious hypothermia victim should not be warmed in the field but should be transported to a hospital medical facility, which can control warming and prevent the shock to the heart of cold, acidic blood. The responsibility of the rescue party is to evacuate the unconscious person as gently as possible. Jarring or bumping the victim may also contribute to heart stoppage.

Tents, sleeping bags, and foam pads provide the best shelter and insulation, but even these must be properly used, and only expedition-quality tents can survive winter storms above tree line; otherwise you must make camp in a sheltered place.

Nylon tarps may provide some protection in a sheltered area, but insulation is required underneath for sitting on the snow. Plastic tarps won't survive in a wind, but they can be used as a ground cloth, or several people can wrap up in one and huddle together for warmth.

Snow caves provide excellent protection, but it takes about two hours to dig a minimal cave for two with a shovel, and even then you must have insulation. With a stove in the party, and thus heat to dry the gear and prepare hot fluid to warm chilled bodies, a snow cave becomes quite livable.

A snow trench or shelter built among living, uncut boughs under a tree are other alternatives, both requiring shovel and tarps to provide any degree of protection in winter. Wind and snow blow through the boughs, but they may help break the wind if you can wrap up in a tarp. A trench will quickly drift full unless there is a good tarp for a roof.

An igloo is excellent shelter but requires more skill to construct than a snow cave. It is also time-consuming and requires a snow saw, perhaps a shovel, and a foam pad. (For more on snow shelters, see Chapter 13.)

Good physical condition is an invaluable deterrent to the "psyching out" that can affect you if you are tired, cold, and lost. Choose companions who are in good condition and choose objectives within your capabilities. To screen out persons who fatigue easily and to work yourself into excellent shape, take short hikes before trying a long, arduous one. If you are with a bunch of tigers it may be possible to persevere through the worst of conditions; if anything goes wrong you are much better off than with a soft group whose members are new at the activity.

Plan what to do if you run late, get lost, or become confused. Assume leadership and force a stop to set up camp before the party is exhausted, cold, and about to collapse. Avoid leading a weak group on a tough trip. It's fine to be the strongest in the party until it becomes a life or death matter, but a close call from an avalanche or storm or a fatality due to your own poor judgment is not easy to live with in the years ahead. Most important, learn when to turn back.

Check the weather. Storm clouds are dismal everywhere. In fact, it's worse in a storm on the inspiring peaks than in the foothill forests. For the high mountains, wait for good weather; you will make miles with less effort and have a view beyond description.

If the temperature is 0°F or colder, be especially careful not to overextend yourself or the group. If you are in cold country where zero is normal, then be extremely careful when the temperature drops to –30°F. Be ready to return to the car if someone is too tired or feet or fingers become too cold.

CLIMATE ADAPTATION

If you are planning a winter trip to a colder range, be prepared for a real shock. For example, if your home area is the "warm" Cascades, then experiencing the bitter cold wind of the eastern mountains is memorable. As much as possible make adequate psychological as well as physical preparation for the blow. Many snowshoe climbs are called off when it gets down to 0°F in the Cascades. It's quite interesting to watch New England climbers on Willy's

© Carl Heilman II/Wild Visions, Inc.

Climbing Gothics in the Adirondacks High Peak Region

Slide at Crawford Notch, New Hampshire, when the temperature is zero and a 10-mph breeze is blowing. The natives will be sitting around comfortably eating lunch without wrapping up in a down jacket. The body I wear has difficulty trying to prepare for zero weather by sitting around at Snoqualmie Pass, Washington, where mixed rain and snow are falling and the temperature is 31.9°F.

It is less painful to adapt to above-freezing weather when you're used to icy temperatures—although even when sweat is running down their faces, people who by long habit wear wool fishnet tops, wool shirt, wool cap, and windbreaker have trouble stripping down for Pacific Coast conditions. Habit makes it difficult to unhook heavy mitts and cord from around their necks, take the water bottle out of their shirts, and stuff both in the pack. Sometimes someone has to tell them to get the windbreaker off and unbutton the wool shirt for ventilation before heat exhaustion becomes a problem.

FROSTBITE

During extremely cold weather a person may freeze the tip of the nose, cheek, ear, finger, or toe during an outing, but unless an entire foot or hand is frozen, this is not too serious. Flesh is damaged first by freezing and then may die of oxygen starvation as blood circulation is cut off. Frostbite is painless. The nerves usually signal for some time that the part is cold, but freezing apparently prevents pain by numbing the nerves, and the only sensation is that the body part is very cold. All snowshoers have cold hands and/or feet some of the time, so it is necessary to check visually for frozen areas. Frostbitten skin is chalky white and the flesh is hard to the touch.

The treatment for frostbite is to restore circulation by thawing the part. Mild surface frostbite or frost nip often can be thawed by contact with warm flesh. When thawed immediately, frost nip does not damage tissue. The tissue may eventually turn brown or blister as from a burn when frozen deeper. Blisters will heal readily unless they are broken, scraped, rubbed, or become infected. Heavy drainage from blisters on a frozen foot or hand that has been thawed will soak up a lot of dressings. Try to keep the area clean; makeshift dressings can be sterilized by scorching material over a flame.

Freezing a hand or foot solid is more serious. Treatment is the same but more difficult due to the extent of the injury. Thawing is done very gently, without rubbing or abrasion. Contrary to the time-honored fallacy, do not rub by hand or with snow; this will tear the blistered flesh and increase damage.

A sheltered place such as a tent, snow cave, or igloo is desirable as working space. Heat water over a stove to about 105°F—just above body temperature—and place the frozen hand or foot in it. Once it is thawed, protect the part from mechanical damage (do not rub it) and especially from refreezing. Bandage and protect it carefully and elevate it to promote circulation.

Before thawing a badly frozen foot, the whole situation must be evaluated. Once

BIGfoot says ▶▶
As a tour leader, I ask others often if any body parts are getting cold. It is much easier to warm up people's parts before they get too cold. Check with each other—it can be fun to warm a friend.

thawed, the victim must not walk out, as pain and tissue damage will be very serious; sled or helicopter evacuation is necessary. However, if evacuation is impossible, and the choice is either to walk out or to sit for perhaps days in a very poor spot, then walk out before the extremity is thawed. Of course, the longer the part is frozen, the greater tissue damage from oxygen starvation will be, but this may be the lesser of two evils. The decision will have to be made on the spot.

Be extremely careful of baring the hands or fingers to manipulate a metal object in subzero temperatures. Cold metal is an excellent conductor of heat from one's fingers—people have gotten frostbitten fingers from picking the car key out of the snow. Also, the metal will freeze to your skin, which will tear when you try to pull away. Be careful, too, when strapping on crampons or handling a stove or fuel bottle. Don't spill subzero fluids such as fuel on your fingers: this is a quick way to get frostbitten. One snowshoer I camped with insisted on a mouthwash to freshen his morning breath, forgetting that the fluid was well below freezing. Fortunately the temperature was not below zero or he would have had frostbite in his mouth.

BIGfoot says ▶▶
The higher the altitude, the more intense the sun's radiation. Add to that the glare off the snow. Three great protectors against the sun are clothing, sunblock, and sunglasses. Use them all!

Tubbs Snowshoe Company

Snowshoeing is a great family outing.

SUNBURN AND WINDBURN

A day, or even a few hours, of sunshine is so delightful in winter that snowshoers may forget its devastating effects on exposed human flesh and eyes, particularly when compounded with reflection from snow—and both effects are made worse at elevations above 8,000 feet. People have even burned the inside of their nostrils or the roof of their mouth. Be sure to carry adequate sun cream or cover with clothing as necessary.

Eyes overexposed to sun or wind will feel as gritty as sandpaper. Protect them with more than adequate sunglasses equipped with side panels, or with goggles that fit over regular glasses or even sunglasses.

Equally painful is windburn, which must be prevented by wearing a face mask.

WIND CHILL AND OVERHEATING

Wind chill factor plays a prominent part in both hypothermia and frostbite. Wind gives the effect of a colder temperature than the thermometer shows. For example, 15°F with a 20-mph wind is equivalent to a temperature of –17°F with no wind. Mountains and ridges do strange things with wind currents. In a sheltered place you may be warm and comfortable, while a hundred feet away a steady wind is blowing and another person is miserable. Clothing should be adaptable to quickly meet changing conditions.

Avoid exposing bare hands for any length of time at low temperatures. A few minutes of subzero temperature with wind is sufficient to turn a nose or cheek white with frost nip. Use a snowshoe binding that does not require removal of mitts. Learn to strap on crampons and close zippers while wearing mitts (a length of cord tied on the zipper pull makes a hold large enough to

> **BIGfoot says ▶▶**
> The layering of clothing allows efficient body temperature regulation. Put on layers to combat cold and wind chill. Take off layers to prevent overheating. (More detailed discussion is in Chapter 5, "Clothing.")

grab with mitts or gloves). Learn to snap photos with mitts on; many Himalayan climbers have frosted their fingers when taking pictures on summits and in their befuddled state of mind did not notice until too late that their fingers would not bend.

Put safety cord on your heavy mitts. One method is to tie a cord to the cuff of each mitt, long enough to be strung around the back of the neck. Attach another cord across your chest to the first cord so that when you remove your pack, cord and mitts can't fall off and/or blow away in the wind.

A second method is to attach a foot-long cord to each mitt with Velcro™ or attach a piece of cloth with a buttonhole to the end of the cord and sew a button on your parka sleeve between the cuff and elbow. The cords are a nuisance on a bushwhack, but the advantage of having them handy in windy subzero weather and not having to stow them in your pack is worth the trouble.

If your hands are easily chilled, take special care of them. If you tend to have cold hands and fingers, use mittens instead of fingered gloves so the fingers can keep each other warm. You can also warm them under armpits—your own or a companion's—before they become dangerously cold. (Some people condition their hands to adapt to the cold by intentionally leaving mitts off as much as possible when working outdoors between winter outings.) Be prepared to cover your face if necessary; wind on a bare face can be painful even if it is not causing frostbite. Don't gasp for breath and risk frostbite in your lungs, mouth, and windpipe during extreme cold conditions.

With a little careful checking at home you can discover whether you are protected from wind. Start at the bottom. The first gap is between boots and pants. You should have tie-down cuffs or gaiters, plus wind pants. Next is the pants-to-shirt gap; a short shirttail won't stay in when you are carrying a pack or bending over. Your underwear or undershirt should cover the waist gap if the shirt doesn't. The wind parka and insulated jacket should extend down to mid-thigh.

Your abdomen and stomach should be protected well, as this is your heat-generating center. Next, the neck and face: can your wind and down parka hoods be cinched tight to leave only nose and goggled eyes out? If not, better make some adjustment. The second layer of protection is the cap face mask, which you should be able to tuck under the lower edge of your goggles. It should cover your nose and mouth and extend down your neck below the shirt collar.

For winter, goggles should have side protection. A cold wind blowing ice particles under ordinary sunglasses and across your eyeballs will have the same effect as snow blindness (sunburn on the surface of the eyes). Wind in your eyes can make them water enough to distort your vision, and tears can freeze in extreme cold. Check your wrists: can you pull down your parka sleeves to cover the wrist of your wool mitts

and seal them with the elastic cuffs? This is desirable, because it is sometimes hard to keep overmitt gauntlets high enough on the forearm to protect the wrist, where the large artery carries warming blood to the hand.

There are a variety of personal styles of dressing for severe wind chill. For example, some people might wear a light balaclava to cover cheeks and chin whenever they are out in winter. When walking into the wind of Mount Washington in New Hampshire at 0°F, a heavy balaclava may be worn on top of the light one, with hood cinched tight and goggles to protect the eyes.

In contrast to wind chill is overheating on sheltered slopes. Cooling is desirable to limit sweating, which dampens clothing and cuts its insulating value. When you are down to one layer, there isn't much more you can remove, therefore it might be wise to back off and slow down to regulate your body temperature and avoid oversweating. If a cold wind blows around the corner, you could chill dangerously fast in clothes wet with sweat.

When you are really snowshoeing hard or the day is warming up, roll up your shirtsleeves, unbutton your shirt, and put your mitts and cap in the pack. This opens up your neck, head, and wrists—where there are many arteries—as well as your chest and belly, to cool air. Some people use fishnet T-shirts and drawers, and unbuttoning the shirt or pants with this string garment underneath does promote cooling. You could also roll up your pant cuffs, unless you will kick too much snow onto your socks. Some people put a 12-inch zipper in the seam of their pants above the knee. This can be opened for more ventilation.

BLISTERS

Some snowshoe bindings can cause blisters, especially if the boot is soft and flexible and cannot withstand the pressure of the binding. First, try adjusting and/or loosening the binding to get relief. Since a snowshoe's weight, when you pick it up to take a step, is on the top of your toes, this is an area that can blister. A piece of foam between boot and binding strap may cushion the foot and provide some relief. Heels suffer on steep sidehills or when climbing steep slopes. Since you cannot effectively edge snowshoes on firm snow, you must walk the way you do on crampons, with the snowshoe flat on the sloping surface and your ankle bent. This is not only tiring but also puts a lot of pressure on the side and back of the heel and on the heel bones.

Take a good supply of adhesive tape, moleskin or adhesive foam, and a few Band-Aids. Cover tender areas with moleskin or tape before they blister. As soon as a tender spot develops, stop and perform first aid. If you use moleskin be sure to take a small scissors or a knife to cut it to fit. After sticking it on, add some strips of adhesive tape to help hold it in place. Once in a while the edge works loose and forms a lump, which makes another blister. If a blister forms, drain it

BIGfoot says ▶▶
Blister prevention starts with petroleum jelly between toes, on top of toes, and on any sensitive places before putting on your socks. As another first line of defense, try soft merino wool socks, along with merino wool sock liners and a proper boot fit.

carefully with a sterile needle and apply moleskin and tape, or apply protection to relieve the pressure and leave the blister to dry. Be careful when you remove the adhesive material at home so it doesn't pull off a large piece of live skin attached beyond the blister. Apply disinfectant if the blister has been abused in this manner.

If a blister is due to a rough spot on the inside of a heavy leather boot, carefully carve the lump smooth with a wood chisel. Smooth all the wrinkles on your socks as you put on your boots, especially when you wear two or more pairs. Check for lumps in the socks, which may be wads of lint.

STOMACH UPSET

Some people on week-long summer backpacks experience some form of mild stomach upset, either vomiting or diarrhea. Both of these can be caused by salmonella from spoiled food residue on cooking pots "going bad." As more people crowd popular recreation sites, coliform and other microbes pollute water supplies. Winter and its cold temperatures protect the backpacker from

some of these problems as living organisms in food residue and water are more or less on hold until it warms up and they can multiply profusely again. Regardless of the season, do not drink from streams. Clean, melted snow, however, is safe to drink. Still, it's best to be prepared. Making several nocturnal dashes from tent to latrine is bad enough in summer, but when it's below zero and breezy and you're camped on a glacier at 9,000 feet with no sheltering trees, it's enough to try one's soul.

Some simple medication doesn't weigh very much in the pack and can help relieve these most uncomfortable problems. Kaopectate™, Alka Seltzer™, Pepto Bismol™, aspirin, and milk of magnesia will ease stomach turmoil. Also, a pair of down or polyester tent booties with leather or rubber soles are a lot faster to get into than double boots when you're in desperate straits. These light boots are quite adequate for a 50-foot dash from the tent—provided you aren't camped on a steep, icy slope. For those who require regular nocturnal strolls, the women are pretty much out of luck, but men can use an extra water bottle (preferably with a special label on it) that has a wide mouth and tight lid—with practice and skill, it can be used as a urinal inside the sleeping bag.

ALTITUDE SICKNESS

People suffer a myriad of miseries when exerting strenuously at elevations that are high in comparison to their home altitude.

Usually the first symptom is fatigue much earlier in the hike than expected, accompanied by hard breathing. Continuing on to increased elevation will likely produce nausea and vomiting and may progress to headache and faintness.

The basic problem is lack of oxygen and barometric pressure, and the problem will usually become noticeable after a thousand feet of elevation gain and especially when reaching around 9,000 to 11,000 feet and above. The most effective treatment is to rest or return to a lower elevation. It takes about two weeks to acclimatize from a near-sea-level altitude to the over-10,000-foot elevations. However, some people don't have that amount of time on a weekend trip, so good judgment and a lot of water and rest, with little or no alcohol, will be your best advice.

The best treatment is to quit doing what is making you sick before you are really miserable. Slow down and don't move so fast that your lungs can't supply enough oxygen to your muscles.

For extra safety, enroll in a mountain-oriented first-aid course for all types of backcountry travel. This knowledge prepares you for those unexpected emergencies. Check with local medical agencies, hospitals, medical clinics, and your local American Red Cross chapter for available courses.

CHAPTER 13

Snow Camping

More care and planning are needed for snow camping than for dry ground camping, which can be as simple as rolling the sleeping bag out under a tree, crawling into it, and going to sleep. Winter camping usually involves a group no smaller than four to six because it takes this many people to break trail for several miles in rough country when conditions are less than ideal—and it's survival by committee.

SHELTER

It might seem that digging a snow cave or building an igloo rather than carrying a tent would save time and energy. But considerable skill and work are necessary to create a snow shelter equal to a light-

weight, roomy, modern tent, and snow in the quantity and consistency required cannot be counted on anyway. The snow cave and igloo really are not practical unless you intend to use them for more than one night or have plenty of time and energy and just want to experiment. Half an hour is plenty of time not only to set up a four-person tent but also to get all four people in it and supper started. Two hours of hard digging by people with average skill is the minimum effort needed to carve out a four-person cave or construct an igloo; realistically, three hours will probably elapse before you can expect to move in. The self-sufficient party has a larger margin of safety. If conditions prevent reaching the desired camping area, or if you get to the right area but the shelter is buried and cannot be found, or you cannot dig your cave or construct an igloo, you still must have shelter. Tents are

◀◀ ▲ *Hoarfrost in the western mountains*

the first choice, especially in somewhat unfamiliar country.

TENTS

A large tent often provides shelter at low per-person weight. If three two-person tents are used, the weight of the tents is from 12 to 15 pounds total, over 2 pounds per person; if rain flies are added, the total weight is almost 3 pounds per person. An 8-pound, four-person tent and a 4-pound, two-person tent average 2 pounds per person. Four people can set up the larger tent about as fast as two people can set up their two-person tent. When conditions are serious, a tarp or tent can shelter double or triple the number of people it was designed to contain.

Knowledge of the area you are going to be in is really helpful. Some excellent camp spots may not have room for a large tent, but small tents can fit in quite well.

Although tents have drawbacks, the 8- to 14-pound weight of a roomy, four-person tent isn't that hard to carry, and the ease and speed of setting it up tip the scales in favor of the tent rather than the snow cave or igloo, unless snow shelters are necessary because the camp site is so windswept that only the most rugged expedition-model tent could survive. For the average snowshoer these tents are too heavy, expensive, and limited in usefulness (see Chapter 6 for more information on tents).

Anchoring tent ropes in snow can be quite a problem. In forested areas it is easy

> **BIGfoot says ▶▶**
> If you are taking a lot of equipment, tools, food, and extra creature comforts for winter camping, why carry it on your back when pulling a sled is much easier? (See Chapter 6 for more on sleds.)

to find a few pieces of dead branch for tent stakes. In unforested areas, be sure to carry your own stakes, for example a $\frac{1}{2}$ x 12–inch dowel, or wood split like kindling. Place these through the loops sewn on the tent, or on the ropes, press or stamp into the snow, and pack snow over them. These small "dead men" anchors are very secure. At times rocks exposed by wind can be used for anchors, although usually such places are too windy for a comfortable camp; the wind popping the fabric interrupts sleep.

Snowshoes and skis also make solid anchors for tent ropes—unless you need them to move around on. At times the snow is so soft that snowshoes are needed to move anywhere outside the tent. Packing the tent platform may be a job, too. After you carefully pack with snowshoes and level the place to pitch the tent, remove the webs and sink in to the knee. Then you pack the platform again by foot. But if you step off the twice-packed spot, you sink in to the hip.

If it is windy and snow is blowing it is necessary to seal the door and put up with condensation. Completely waterproof fabrics in this situation prevent any moisture from passing through the fabric and can cause near-rainfall conditions within the tent. Carry a sponge with your tent supplies for mopping up the condensation and any other wet messes that might happen. Enough snow to wet the top of your bag can blow in through a zipper that is not completely closed.

Camping in wet weather in winter may seem foolish, but it may happen unplanned. The weather may be sunny when you start out, but before the day is over a storm moves in and you have to stay the night. Too, the storm may pass through and the next day will be fine. Sometimes it may be cloudy and wet in the valleys, but up high, above 10,000 feet, the weather is cold and clear. Then it is practical to put up with a day or two of storm to get to the higher scenic area where it's sunny and dry. There are times when some members of the group are so ardent there is no way to talk them out of starting on the trip even in near-blizzard conditions. Only when they are sufficiently wet, cold, and miserable do they accept the fact that an outing in a winter storm truly can be worse than no outing at all.

SNOW CAVES

Snow caves provide the maximum protection from storm but are time-consuming and tiring to construct. The usual problem is that the excavators get tired before there is really enough room to be comfortable. It's a bad day when you must dig your first cave ever and spend the night in it, and it is 8:00 P.M. and dark before you start.

Obviously, careful thought must be given to the location for a snow cave so nothing

BIGfoot says ▶▶
When making snow caves and igloos, stop traveling early enough so site selection and construction won't have to be hurried. Remember that you are out there to have fun.

will fall on it and snow won't drift over and seal you in. During a mountain rescue training session in the southern Washington Cascades, some participants decided to dig their caves on the lee side of a ridge. The windward side was packed too hard, besides having a wind and drifting problem. The lee slope was not steep, it leveled out below, and it was out of the wind, so a whole string of caves was started side by side to house thirty or more persons. Real progress was being made, as the snow was deep, soft enough to dig well, but not so soft that a cave roof would fall in. To the surprise of the entire group, the slope avalanched; the tunneling had cut loose a slab avalanche, which carried the mountain rescue people a short distance down the slope. Among the many things to be considered in the location of the caves, avalanche hazard was the only thing overlooked in this otherwise ideal spot. If you have a choice between a flat spot sheltered by trees or an open slope where the digging is easy, be sure to consider avalanche hazard before deciding to spend the night on the slope.

Some locations are less satisfactory than others for snow caves, a flat place being the worst. First, you have to excavate a hole straight down. When the hole is deep enough—6 feet or so—one person must tunnel in horizontally to create the room, while someone else tosses the snow up out of the original hole. A slope is useful because the snow dug out falls out of the way. Usually some of the last of it must be thrown out by a second person because as the cave reaches a depth of 6 to 8 feet the shovel operator cannot throw the chunks out beyond the entrance. A snowshoe makes an excellent tool for the second shoveler.

Two items are handy for actual construction: a snow shovel and either a snow saw or a folding pruning saw. An excellent shovel can be made by cutting off the blade of an aluminum grain scoop shovel so it is 12 inches long; if longer it will hold too much snow. Small aluminum snow shovels are poor tools for digging a snow cave but will suffice in the absence of the heavier grain scoop shovel (more on shovels in Chapter 6). A folding pruning saw is lightweight and in some instances can be used to cut through an ice layer that a shovel cannot dent.

It might also be efficient to carry good rain gear, extra mitts, and possibly some thick rubber gloves in anticipation of this wet job.

There is a real technique to digging that far into snow. Of course, the snow depth must be a foot or more deeper than the cave is high; too shallow a roof, less than 12 to 18 inches, may collapse. The snow at the bottom and rear of the cave may have settled so that the shovel can be jabbed only a couple of inches into it. Then each chunk must be chipped loose on three sides and pried off the wall. Too much pressure can easily bend cheap, lightweight, aluminum shovels. Make sure you purchase a shovel that has been designed to do the job, not merely paw loose snow around. However, it is possible to study the mechanics of the problem and develop a technique to dislodge the most material with the least effort without breaking the shovel. A shortened grain scoop is quite strong and superb for this job. This is digging at its worst, reaching overhead as well as underfoot and working in awkward positions. Even more discouraging is encountering a stump or mound of dirt that forces excavation in a different direction.

It is much better to find a slope and to tunnel straight in. Some diagrams show a very low opening with a high-domed room beyond (Figure 32). The problem with this design is digging through the small opening on your knees or lying down. For speed, make the door high enough to dig in a fairly comfortable stance. Snow caves need plenty of ventilation, which the high door provides. Take a small plastic or nylon tarp to hang in the doorway. This will be adequate to keep the weather out unless there is a real storm raging, in which case

Figure 32. Snow cave construction

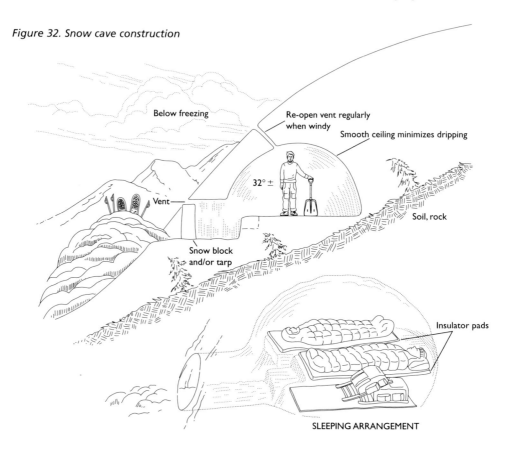

Below freezing

Re-open vent regularly when windy

Smooth ceiling minimizes dripping

32° ±

Vent

Soil, rock

Snow block and/or tarp

Insulator pads

SLEEPING ARRANGEMENT

you may want to develop a deeper, more elaborate cave.

The cave is different from a tent in that you cannot bulge the wall out with an elbow or shoulder. If you touch the wall, snow trickles down onto your sleeping bags or clothing. Foam pads are the best insulation on the floor. Some pads are so lightweight that you may be tempted to carry several to better cover the floor of the cave, which somehow always turns out to be lumpy and hard.

Self-inflating air/foam combination mattresses give a superb cushion to the otherwise surprisingly hard snow floor. However, for subzero temperatures it is usually necessary to add some insulation to the mattress. They are made warmer with an additional layer of lightweight foam pad.

Once in a while it is possible to spend enough time with a good shovel to dig a cave with plenty of elbow, sleeping, and cooking room. The first such luxurious cavern I observed had a very low entrance so all heat was trapped in the smoothly domed chamber. But the instructional diagram had showed no vent hole. As supper was cooked on the gas stove, the oxygen became exhausted to the extent that the one heavy smoker in the group nearly fainted. Realizing the cause, all bailed out and soon recovered. A hole was poked through the ceiling, releasing some warmth along with carbon dioxide, carbon monoxide, and various cooking odors, and admitting oxygen.

A cave such as this is a luxury, since sounds such as wind are stilled, giving a real sense of security to those within. Not all sounds are muted, however. Another cave I occupied had several drawbacks. The first was that we had not intended to dig it, but the February snow was so deep that we could not find the Forest Service shelter we had intended to use. So we dug a cave in a flat area because there was no convenient slope. We also dug into a tree and left a branch sticking out from one wall, which dripped water onto one sleeping bag all night. Trees outside were so loaded with snow from the storm that from time to time a branch would droop low and the immense snow load would slide off, landing with a loud whoomp! At intervals this muffled thud would awaken me so I could consider the difficulty of digging out of a collapsed snow cave. The task would probably have been impossible with several feet of snow packed around me and the sleeping bag zipped up to my nose. Simpler one-person caves and trenches are shown in Figures 33 and 34.

IGLOOS

Igloos are equal in protection to snow caves but more than equal in the skill required to construct them (Figure 35). They are also more subject to snow conditions. Wet, packing snow has the advantage that the blocks stick together and stay in place well, but are quite heavy. Often there are weak layers that make it hard to cut large blocks. Wind-packed dry snow is the easiest to work with. Weight is not excessive and even large blocks are strong, do not break easily, and are easy to lift.

Figure 33.
One-person cave for
shallow snow depth.
Stomp snow first,
excavate three
tunnels, then
connect the tunnels.

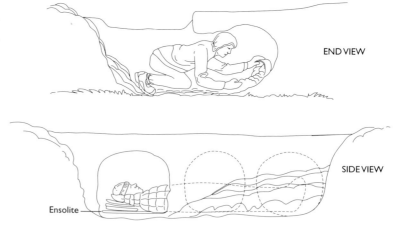

Figure 34. One- or
two-person covered
trench

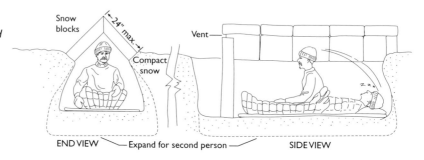

Often an area of dry snow must be packed with snowshoes before it can be cut into blocks. Walk it down evenly, then eat lunch and allow it twenty to thirty minutes to harden. Don't try for more compaction by removing snowshoes because bare boots will punch holes and pack the snow unevenly, causing poor-quality blocks. A beginner with even, consistent blocks to work with can construct a good-looking, solid igloo.

Under ideal conditions an expert can whip up a four-person structure in about half an hour. As with a snow cave, any snow butcher with a minimum of skill and enough persistence can build an igloo. Generally allow three hours or so for the job unless you have perfected your skill through practice. Two snow saws speed the work—one for the person cutting blocks and the other to carefully tailor each block to fit the two surfaces it will touch. A shovel is also helpful; if only one saw is available, a shovel can be used for either cutting blocks or fitting them. Some people prefer a carpenter's saw to either snow saw or shovel.

One expert igloo builder advises a homemade snow saw of the following specifications: use a piece of tempered 7075 aluminum alloy about $\frac{1}{8}$-inch thick, 2 inches wide, and 26 inches long. Attach a wooden handle to one end, leaving 20 inches for the cutting blade. Use a hacksaw to cut serrations in it for the teeth. This allows you to cut blocks up to 20 inches high, making it possible to dome over the igloo roof in about four tiers of blocks.

Cut the first tier at a slant so that the second tier will spiral up. Cut the door out after the wall is somewhat above it, since it is hard to cut out a block long enough to extend across the door opening and strong enough to support the wall above. Bevel the top of each tier to slope the walls inward toward the top of the dome. (Actually, a cone-shaped igloo, with nearly straight walls, is easier to construct than a rounded dome.) If the top of each tier is horizontal, you will end up with nearly vertical sidewalls and have trouble drawing them in to close the top. The person laying blocks must work within the circle as the tiers rise. Some prefer to cut blocks from the floor, excavating a foot or more of depth, which cuts down on the height of blocks to be laid. Ideal size for the blocks is about 12 x 18 x 6 inches. Uniformity

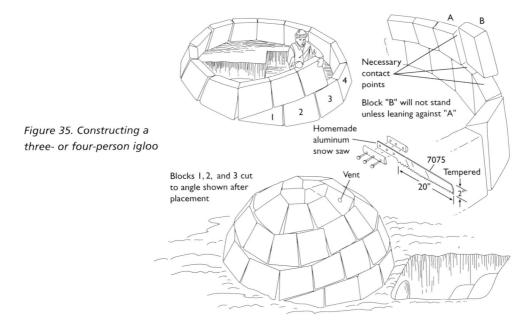

Figure 35. Constructing a three- or four-person igloo

Necessary contact points

Block "B" will not stand unless leaning against "A"

Homemade aluminum snow saw

7075 Tempered

20"

Blocks 1, 2, and 3 cut to angle shown after placement

Vent

depends more on the block cutter's skill than the condition of the snow, but the more uniform the size and shape of the blocks, the easier it is to lay them in position. Layers, especially of ice, in the snow can cause blocks to come apart. Don't try to build too high, as it is difficult to fit a block if you must raise it much above shoulder level. The keystone, or capstone, block must leave an opening for ventilation; this is less of a problem than in a snow cave but still necessary. People with less than expert skill usually have no problem with ventilation. Poorly fitted blocks leave holes that make the igloo look like a Halloween jack-o'-lantern with a lot of eyes and mouths.

As in snow caving, rubber gloves are useful; long gauntlets will keep snow from working into the cuffs of your sleeves as the last blocks are raised to position. All chinks must be caulked. With powder snow it may be desirable to melt water and splash some on any weak places. An entrance tunnel may be built, although most people are ready to quit before then. A plastic tarp may be rigged to cover the opening, especially if held in place by packs on the inside.

The inside surface must have no points from which moisture can drip. The greatest disadvantage of snow shelters becomes obvious when temperatures rise above freezing. The ceiling drips, especially at the top of the door and the vent hole. The humid air may be saturated by vapor from boiling water, stove emissions, and the breath of the occupants. Remember to bring along a sponge to sop up all the water. The interior of the igloo is illuminated by light filtering through; if light is visible through the ceiling of a snow cave, it is too thin and may fall in. The white walls of both cave and igloo reflect light so well that one flashlight or candle is usually adequate for lighting.

OTHER SHELTERS

Other types of snow shelters include a dug **trench** roofed with snowshoes or dead branches and a tarp covered with snow. Long snow blocks may be tilted together to roof over the trench (Figure 34). It is a good idea to be familiar with several of these shelters. In some places and conditions where it is impossible to use one type, another will work.

The permanent **log** and **stone shelters** erected by the Forest Service or Park Service are excellent in winter, providing protection that cannot be matched by tents or snow shelters. However, **tents** should be carried on backpacks to distant backcountry or high, isolated peaks even though there may be a permanent shelter at the desired camp spot. Sometimes conditions—storm, rugged snowshoeing, or delays due to people—prevent a party from reaching the shelter location. Without tents the unintentional overnight bivouac may be a real disaster.

No matter how fast you can put up the tent, dig the cave, or build the igloo, allow plenty of time for the job. Tent ropes become tangled; the weather and/or snow may be uncooperative. Winter days are short. At 47° north latitude the sun sets at 3:30 P.M. during the dark, dismal season of late December to mid-January. Heavy cloud cover further cuts the limited daylight available, and some deep valley bottoms have no direct sunlight from mid-November until early February.

Be aware of these damp, cold spots and prepare for them. Cold air settles to the valley bottoms in such shaded areas. Sometimes it is much warmer a hundred feet or so up the south-facing hillside. It may be worthwhile to make a short climb out of the valley bottom to camp in a warmer spot. The most ideal summer camping spot will be the place to avoid in the winter—summer campers want a cool spot and winter campers want a warmer one.

FIRES

For emergencies and in lowland forest areas where dead trees abound, a fire may be a possibility during snow camping. In many areas trees are scarce and scenic and should not be used unless it really is an emergency and life, rather than comfort, depends on a fire.

Starting a fire in winter is not always easy, and again preparation is the key. Practice on day hikes. Carry a piece of candle, a firestarter made of rolled newspaper soaked in paraffin wax, or pitch wood. Break off a good supply of small dead twigs from near the bottom of a tree trunk; these are usually kept dry by sheltering live branches above. You might also find drops of dried sap that will burn like pitch and can help initial efforts to start a fire. Occasionally you may find a dead tree with an abundance of dry, dead branches, but this is rare. Ignite a pile of twigs with the firestarter and add larger pieces of wood, being careful to keep the flame going. A fuzz stick—a dry piece of wood with shavings carved in it—is an alternative where dry twigs are unavailable. A fire-resistant platform must be provided to keep the fire from melting down into the snow. A piece of light sheet metal, hinged to fold small enough to fit in a pack, is ideal. It may be suspended above the snow by baling wire attached to trees or with stakes driven into the snow. Cut green wood to build the fire on only in case of an emergency to actually save a life, as living trees are too valuable to cut and burn for a mere marshmallow roast. A length of plastic or rubber tubing is an old standby that is handy for blowing on the kindling to provide a draft. The extended draft gives the flame a boost, while sparing your face from soot and lungs from smoke.

BIGfoot says ▶▶
Firestarters include strike-anywhere matches cut to fit in sealed film canisters, disposable lighters, a magnifying glass, and short candles (wrapped in foil) to light other material. Starting materials can include fine steel wool, clothes-dryer filter lint, shredded waxed paper, dry wood shavings, or even a piece of your cotton shirttail.

If you can get flames started in an area about 6 inches across, a fire will probably go. By the time the flames cover about a square foot and have a good bed of coals, good-size pieces of fairly wet wood may be added; the heat will dry them and the fire will continue burning. Sometimes desperate methods must be used—such as carrying a pint of gasoline, a highway flare, or a half-pound of old inner tube—to get the blaze going. Many outdoor manuals show solid fuel tablets and other firestarters. But for real performance under difficult circumstances these are inadequate for the job at hand.

Most surefire aids are as heavy as a stove. It is usually hard to get a fire going under winter conditions, even when fairly dry, dead branches or dry twigs are available. At times it may be impossible because moisture in the air has saturated even dead wood. Some areas just do not have enough firewood for the number of people who camp there. Generally it is not practical or desirable to depend on using a wood fire. But don't let the old-time woodsman skill at starting a fire die out. An emergency may arise when a huge heat source such as a generous bonfire would mean surviving well for several days.

STOVES AND COOKING

Although open fires are not practical in a snow cave or igloo, cooking over a stove in a tent is not easy either, and it can be dangerous. I don't suggest it, even though sometimes I know it might have to be done. At least set up near the door for quick evacuation. Extra care must be taken to clear a place large enough to set up the stove. Any spillage of fuel or food can land on the sleeping bags or on the floor, making frequent house-cleaning necessary. For this reason it is a good idea to use a simple menu for meals when conditions such as storm or extreme cold or a predawn start make it necessary to cook inside the shelter.

The greatest problem in tent house-keeping is melting snow for water. You will need a large pot to hold the necessary volume of snow. Potential disasters develop when a gallon of water is perched on top of a half-pint stove, especially when the ingredients for dinner have been added. Dumping snow in the pot usually leaves some dribbles of snow from the tent door to the pot on the stove. Dipping hot water from the container adds more drops to the tent floor. If the stove is set on the floor without an insulating pad or piece of plywood under it, melting snow underneath may slowly tip the water pot off the burner.

A coated-nylon stuff sack large enough to hold a sleeping bag and with no leaks can make the snow-melting process easier. Fill the sack with snow, brush the snow off the outside, and bring it into the tent or shelter. You can then carefully ladle the snow into the melting pot with minimum spillage and only one trip outside.

You'll learn certain techniques to cook over a small stove in cramped quarters.

Limited heat on a single burner dictates that one course be prepared and consumed at a time. The time and bother required to melt snow for water generally prompts people to choose a one-course, one-dish meal. The simplest method is to melt the snow, heat the water, and pour it into individual containers to reconstitute some dehydrated or freeze-dried food. Add more snow to the pot, and by the time you eat your first course, more hot water is available. If someone is still hungry, fix another round, and add more snow to the pot. As each person finishes eating, use the hot water for cocoa, tea, powdered juice, or coffee and to rinse the food residue from your cup.

Replacing the traditional can of pork and beans, the new dehydrated foods are lightweight, simple, and fast to reconstitute. They can be costly, however, especially items that are packaged in individual servings. Read the directions carefully, as some require only boiling water, some are best when added to another ingredient, and others must be soaked then fried. Read the labels carefully at home to be sure you pack enough utensils.

Great progress has been made in lighter processed foods, but despite the exotic names on the package, the flavor is uniformly drab and monotonous without additional seasoning. Backpackers have little choice, as the alternative is prohibitive weight or starvation. But cold temperatures and availability of snow for refrigeration give snowshoers the option of including uncooked meat, frozen foods, and

> **BIGfoot says ▶▶**
> To liven up otherwise bland foods, put several of your favorite spices—pepper, garlic, cinnamon, salt, or chili powder—wrapped individually in plastic-baggie corners stuffed in a film canister.

other perishables in the menu. However, these items are so heavy they are likely to be used only as a delicious respite from the processed mainstay.

Encourage ingenuity in menu planning. Mountain snowshoers have revolutionized snowshoe design and technique—it's about time someone did something about the food.

GARBAGE AND WASTE

It is easy to forget that the blanket of snow that covers all ugliness will melt away and reveal every tin can and candy wrapper left by thoughtless winter campers. The message is brief and admits no exceptions: if you can carry it in full, you can carry it out empty.

Human wastes cannot be buried in topsoil as they should be in summer, but can be buried under the snow, so choose as unobtrusive a location as possible, such as the depths of a clump of trees, and, whenever possible, burn the used toilet paper. (The amount of yellow snow along popular snow hikes does not enhance the backcountry beauty. Make the effort to get off the trail, out of sight, and cover it up.)

CHAPTER 14

Snowshoe Running and Racing

Most of the information in the previous chapters has dealt with snowshoeing for hiking and backpacking while battling the elements and terrain in the backcountry. Snowshoeing has also become increasingly popular among runners, joggers, and those who cross-train in numerous other sports who are looking for new types of aerobic fitness exercise. Across the Snow Belt from coast to coast, winter has frustrated many serious runners and fitness joggers. Runners and joggers who discover showshoeing find that they can continue their training and conditioning throughout the winter months.

As the first snowshoe clubs started forming in the late 1700s to early 1800s and meeting more and more challenges, snowshoe racing evolved, too. By the early 1900s, organized competition in the north-

BIGfoot says ▶▶

For fitness devotees used to dry land, low altitude, and flatter running and racing terrain, "running" and "racing" may be only figures of speech while on snowshoes. Add higher altitude, the extra weight of snowshoes and winter gear, the resistance of the snow, and hills and you might find that on snowshoes a "power hike" is more than enough.

eastern United States and Canada on oval tracks for measured distances led to the establishment of rules, records, and the use of limited sizes and shapes of snowshoes attached by only certain kinds of binding and without claws. These types of races—although less popular than they were years ago—are still being staged today.

Now more popular for most snow country racing is a course planned on

◀◀ ▲ *Mountain trail runners race on snow-shoes in winter.*

snow-covered trails, logging roads, and routes left to the imagination. Snowshoe tracks may travel over rolling hills, up and down steep mountain trails, through the next valley, and for any length desired— and not necessarily accurately measured. One race may be on a prepared and packed route, while another will depend on fresh, deep powder and may even require a few navigational skills if you are in the front of the pack.

Race organizers with creativity, and sometimes a little sense of humor, will combine terrain and conditions, then add a few more obstacles for the challenge. Race

BIGfoot says ▶▶
In some snowshoe races, you had better know the way if you are in the lead. If you are back in the pack, you should just follow the track.

names are as unique as the routes themselves: Beargrease Marathon; Woodchuck Shuffle; Off Track, Off Beat; Jingle Bell Run; Frost Fever; and the In and Out of Luck New World Championships. One popular race is patterned after Alaska's famous sled-dog race, the Iditarod. It's called the Iditashoe, and it is 100 miles long! If you are in the Anchorage area in February and looking for some fun or a race, check with the locals and join in the competition.

A few organizers have tried to establish snowshoe-racing standards, as road-running athletes have done. A number of obstacles seem to slow down such organizational attempts. The independent attitude of snowshoers, which gets them outside in the cold of winter, may make it hard to agree on rules for developing a long-lasting governing body. Measured courses can be consistent in distance, but not in snow- or

Redfeather Snowshoe Company

Frank Shorter (left), 1972 Olympic marathon winner, and Tom Sobal, snowshoe race organizer, champion, and burro racer, on training run at Brainard Lake on the edge of Indian Peaks Wilderness, Colorado (10,300-foot elevation)

weather-related conditions, so time and distance records would be far too dependent on these variable conditions rather than the athletes' own abilities. A course that might take the winner one hour to complete on one day might take the same racer two hours the next day just because of a change in weather and snow conditions. The statistics for each race have to be good only for that day with no comparisons really possible to another year or a similar course.

The United States Snowshoe Association (USSSA), which was founded by George and Candice Bosworth in 1977, has been a major force in trying to standardize and regulate snowshoe racing. There was finally a first annual U.S. Championship Race in 2002, after four qualifying regional races. The four regions are designated the Northeastern, North Central, Rocky Mountain, and Western. The distances may range from 5 to 15 kilometers, with a top number of qualifiers going to the nationals.

At this writing, the size or displacement area for the minimum-size snowshoes allowed is about to be formulated. The hope will be to at least have exhibition events for the 2006 Winter Olympic Games in Italy.

In Quebec, Ontario, and New England some races are still run according to the rules of the Canadian Snowshoe Union and the American Snowshoe Union. This is sometimes described as the French Canadian and Franco-American style of snowshoe racing. The unions exist partly to preserve the wood-frame, babiche (rawhide) laced snowshoe used with the lampwick, or squaw hitch, binding. These special racing snowshoes, weighing 19 ounces, are the lightest of any used for racing. A 9 x 32–inch size is used for running and a 10 x 32–inch for race walking, or hard walking. No cleats or traction devices are permitted on either size.

Representatives of the Canadian and American snowshoe unions have combined to form the International Snowshoe Union. This body has established their rules for competition, including the number and location of annual events. They also resolve any disputes or disagreements.

Races may include runs of 50, 100, 200, 400, and 800 meters; 1,500-meter, 1-mile,

Redfeather Snowshoe Company

When racing at high altitudes and in deep snow, use poles for more balance and power.

and 10-mile hard walks; and 100-meter hurdles. Both men and women compete in several age groups. Many clubs within the International Snowshoe Union sponsor races and social gatherings. Each club has a uniform, usually a heavy wool coat and pants, with distinctive colors and names. Sweat clothes and running shoes are accepted clothing for meets. Previously, racers wore heavy club uniforms and moccasins.

The races are usually held on somewhat prepared courses—often snow-covered running tracks—packed down or churned

---

BIGfoot says ▶▶

The modern snowshoes designed for running and racing are shorter and lighter, have fixed-hinge bindings (a shin saver), and are sometimes asymmetrical in shape (see Chart 2, Chapter 2).

Photos by BIGfoot Fotos

It's crowded at the race start.

The strong take the lead on the uphills.

up depending on the temperature and type of snow. When the International Snowshoe Union Convention was held in Ottawa in 1975, streets were closed for the race course and snow trucked in because a warm spell had bared the pavement.

Adapting to the weather is a major challenge each year for snowshoe-racing organizers. When snow falls early and stays on the ground a long time, more meets will be scheduled. Poor snow cover—or no snow at all—shortens the racing season. Sometimes the snow melts early, in which case races may be run on the previous year's dead grass. Racing is more sensitive to lack of snow than recreational snowshoeing. Mountain heights receive more snow than valley floors, but you can't move the races to mountain ridges and summits!

Snowshoers in the upper Midwest—Wisconsin, Michigan, and Minnesota—seem to prefer a somewhat different racing style:

longer distances on a cross-country ski course. Local community races have been held for years, and an 80-mile race sponsored by a distillery has created even more interest.

Long snowy winters and cold temperatures are nearly synonymous with this region. The Midwest racing style is less structured than that of other racing groups in regard to equipment and distance. Longer distances on a cross-country ski course are the norm for length, and Western metal-framed snowshoes, usually a minimum size of 8 x 25 inches, for equipment. Some of the specially designed lightweight racing models may be as small as 7 x 24 inches or 8 x 22 inches (see Chart 2, Chapter 2). Because of the soft snow on many courses, some racers often use larger snowshoes. At times snowshoe races are run on packed snow that is nearly as hard as ice, where a runner without snowshoes would be faster. However, some races are run half on groomed cross-country courses and half through the woods and up and down hills. Sometimes trail breaking is required, and snowshoes are necessary to keep from sinking too deeply.

In the northern Adirondacks, the Paul Smith College Striders have a tradition of snowshoe running for training and competition, and host a series of races, including the North American Snowshoe Classic. The events have been the 8,000-meter cross-country run, 200- and 400-meter sprints, and a 1,500-meter walk. When these events are hosted in Quebec, it is called the Classique Nord Americaine de la Raquette. The Empire State Winter Games at Lake Placid, New York, have been a major event, with skiing, skating, and snowshoe racing.

As if running on snowshoes at sea level isn't challenging enough, a roster of races is scheduled in Colorado at 10,000 feet or so. In one race, snowshoers trek to the top of Colorado's highest peak, Mount Elbert (14,433 feet), and down again. Some races at high altitudes are short distances; however, a growing number are longer distances, 5 and 10 kilometers and more. In a way this is appropriate, because snow doesn't lend itself to high-speed travel except downhill on skis. The long-term ethic for races on snow seems to be more in the nature of long distances and endurance. Snowshoe racing has also been combined with other sports, such as cross-country skiing, running, bicycling, or ice skating, to form biathlons, triathlons, and quadathlons.

BiGfoot Fotos

Tom Sobal in the off season

The snowshoes used are the same as discussed above for Midwestern races.

The stress of running in cold weather is no drawback to people who love running and competing. I entered the 1,500-meter race walk at the 1991 North American Snowshoe Classic at Gabriels, New York, and at age sixty-two I was twenty years older than the next oldest racer, so was obviously no threat to anyone. I warmed up prior to the race since cold muscles are easily strained or torn, then I was ready to go.

Of the seventeen people—male and female—in my race, only two or three were serious athletes. The rest were capable of varying degrees of speed, and seven were less serious or speedy than this old farmer! This seems to be fairly typical of most such races. The socializing with people from the opposite side of the continent was more rewarding than the athletic achievement.

Snowshoe racing is very different from snowshoeing while hiking and backpacking in the mountains. A westerner would never run out of new mountain areas to snowshoe. However, the limited extent of eastern mountains causes local snowshoers to repeat climbs, sometimes frequently. One very active snowshoer has in winter trekked up all forty-six New England summits over 4,000 feet and ascended nearly all of them from all four points of the compass. It's not surprising that snow-shoe racing has grown in popularity in the Midwest and the East, where winters are long and subzero temperatures tend to discourage backpackers from camping in the backcountry.

Another kind of snowshoe racing—winter mountain rescue practice—has developed in Washington State. Several have been sponsored by Ellensburg Mountain Rescue. The simulated rescue format calls for a "victim" to be evacuated in a rescue sled off a nontechnical mountain summit (no mountaineering required), which includes an elevation gain of 3,000 feet. The winning team is the first to complete the three-hour round trip.

For more information on snowshoe racing, demonstration days, fun festivals, clubs, and organizations, contact hiking stores and snowshoe retail outlets in your area.

Appendix 1: Equipment Checklist

Many items in this list need no description in the text. By the time most people are ready to try snowshoeing, they have acquired some knowledge and equipment, and general suggestions should be adequate. If you need more information, refer to the excellent books in the Suggested Reading list.

The following checklist is not intended to be definitive. Other items may be equally satisfactory—the last word on snowshoeing equipment has yet to be written. Try your own ideas, improvise, and modify. There is plenty of room for improvement.

Not all items need be taken on all trips. On an easy, short hike some items may be excluded. For longer hikes where a delay could force an overnight stay, start adding the items listed under Group and Optional.

Snowshoe groups usually stay together because the stronger members cannot outrun the weaker ones when breaking trail through deep snow. A tired person cannot be left to sit beside the trail for several hours in 10°F weather while the rest of the party continues on to the destination. Therefore some items may be shared within a group, such as map and compass and, to a lesser extent, first-aid supplies. Make sure someone else has the items you plan to leave home. Even experienced people sometimes inadvertently overlook such necessities as matches.

Ski poles fully occupy both hands, and even with an ice ax, a headlamp-type flashlight is more practical than a handheld one. Headlamps that use a 6- or 4.5-volt battery last longer and beam more focused light than older two-cell models and are strongly recommended. Lithium-cell lights are the lightest-weight and longest-lived lights available. The new light-emitting-diode (LED) headlamps are extremely lightweight and efficient; they use three AAA batteries and do not consume much energy. Cold temperature shortens battery life and short days require more flashlight use, so equip yourself better than you would in summer.

Add one stove per group for a hot drink during rest stops. Don't skimp on matches and firestarter if you intend to build a fire; remember that dry wood is scarce or nonexistent during winter so it is unwise to depend on a fire. Carry a knife with a leather punch and add a saw to group equipment. Shovel and snow saw are optional; their necessity will depend on the length of the trip and risk of an overnight stay on one-day trips.

Extra food is of less importance because the risk of starvation during an overnight stay is slight, but the risk of hypothermia and/or frostbite is very high if you are caught in a storm without much shelter. Some of the small emergency kits contain a tea bag, bouillon, and sugar cubes as extra food. These items won't do much to prolong life; their chief purpose is to help pass the unpleasant hours more easily and to improve the taste of wood-ash-flavored melted snow.

As you gain experience from snowshoeing in different conditions, deciding what to put in your pack will be less of a problem. Equipment that is desirable on a subzero outing will not be necessary for a mid-May, 60°F hike. If there are beginners along, be sure to check that everyone has the essentials, and take the time and effort to help the first-timers shake down their equipment.

Plan your equipment creatively and don't depend blindly on any checklist. Improvise and experiment so that your equipment will meet the varying conditions you find in your area without unnecessary fussing and adjusting. If the gear you have doesn't work, learn to make it work or replace it. Don't spend your outdoor time changing clothes and tightening or loosening straps and buckles. Enjoy the winter backcountry to the fullest while you are there.

DAY HIKE

CLOTHING
(Minimum number of layers necessary to adjust to anticipated weather conditions)

Long underwear—(layer 1) top and bottom of polypropylene, polyester, or wool

Pants—(layer 2) loose-fitting, wool, nylon, polyester, and/or blends

Upper body—(layer 2 and 3) polyester fleece or pile shirts or sweaters (wool shirts for the traditionalists)

Outer shell—top and bottom usually of nylon; treated, coated, or laminated to be wind- and water-repellent/proof; pants preferably with full leg zippers; top with a hood

Socks—medium- to heavyweight wool over a liner sock of light wool and/or polypropylene/polyester blend (be sure to allow enough room for these when fitting your boots); extra socks in case of wet feet

Boots—light hiking or mountaineering boots, pac boots, or winter sport boots

Gaiters—to keep snow out of boots

Headgear—wool or fleece cap and face mask or combination; and/or billed cap with ear flaps; hood of outer shell

Mittens—wool or polyester fleece with overmitts, with extras and glove liners

THE TEN ESSENTIALS

1. Map—a topographic map of the area with protective covering or plastic bag
2. Compass—know how to use it with the map (altimeter and GPS optional)
3. Sunglasses and sunscreen—protection from sunlight and glare off snow
4. Extra food and water—for beyond the expected excursion time for emergency situations
5. Extra clothing—as the layers discussed above for changing weather conditions, including extra mittens and caps
6. Headlamp/flashlight—with extra battery power and spare bulb
7. First-aid supplies—small, compact kits; keep in waterproof/plastic bag
8. Firestarter—for emergencies requiring more than matches or lighters
9. Matches—in waterproof container, and plenty of them
10. Knife—with blades and tools

EQUIPMENT

Snowshoes
Backcountry snowshoe/ski poles or ice ax with basket
Backpack
The Ten Essentials (listed above)
Repair kit for snowshoes and equipment (cord, cable ties, tape, safety pins, etc., plus knife/tool)
Signaling devices (plastic whistle and mirror)
Space blankets (2)

Add, per group:
Flagging (engineer's tape)
Wands (with flagging attached, 25 or more if route is intricate or long)
Folding saw
Shovels (minimum of 2 per group)
Plastic or nylon tarps (1 or 2, for emergency overnight stay)

If weather is 10°F or colder, add or change to:
Extra-warm clothing in layers; i.e., fleece, pile, outer gear
Down mitts or especially warm insulated mitts, equipped with safety cord to prevent loss in wind
Expedition overboots over heavy climbing or double boots
Stove and pot for hot drinks and heavy-duty firestarter

For avalanche country:
Radio avalanche victim detectors (1 for each party member)

Shovels (1 per person)
Avalanche probes (2 or more per group)
Avalanche cord—50 to 100 feet per person (especially if detectors are not available)

Special for subzero outings:

Quart water bottle with wide neck in pack next to your back
Quart or pint bottle with wide neck inside shirt, equipped with neck cord for easier retrieval from shirt front (the openings of narrow-neck bottles can freeze if exposed)
Extra socks and mitts

For an overnight trip, add:

Snorkel (optional)
Down-filled tent slippers (optional)
Adequate sleeping bag
Foam pad (2; optional)
Sleeping-bag liner
Cup, spoon, and cooking utensils as needed

Hot breakfast and dinner, with hot drink
Cold lunch (optional; stop to heat water for hot drink on trail)

For the group:

Tent or tents (adequate space for entire group)
Snow anchors
Rain fly (optional)
Plastic or nylon tarp or large garbage sack (for storing packs and gear outside if there is not enough room in tents)
Stove, extra fuel, pot large enough to melt snow
Base for stove or metal fire platform
Shovel, snow saw (for leveling tent platform or digging cave or building igloo)
Whisk broom (for brushing snow off boots and gear brought into tent)
Sponge (for wiping up drips and spills)

Appendix 2: Suggested Reading

American Outdoor Safety League. *Emergency Survival Handbook,* 4th ed. Seattle: The Mountaineers Books, 1987.

Armstrong, Betsy R., Knox Williams, and Richard L. Armstrong. *The Avalanche Book.* Golden, Colo.: Fulcrum Publishing, 1992.

Bezruchka, Stephen. *Altitude Illness: Prevention and Treatment.* Seattle: The Mountaineers Books, 1994.

Carline, Jan D., Martha J. Lentz, and Steven C. Macdonald. *Mountaineering First Aid: A Guide to Accident Response and First Aid Care,* 4th ed. Seattle: The Mountaineers Books, 1996.

Fleming, June. *Staying Found: The Complete Map and Compass Handbook,* 3rd ed. Seattle: The Mountaineers Books, 2001.

Graydon, Don, and Kurt Hanson, editors. *Mountaineering: The Freedom of the Hills,* 6th ed. Seattle: The Mountaineers Books, 1997.

La Chapelle, Edward R. *The ABC of Avalanche Safety,* 2nd ed. Seattle: The Mountaineers Books, 1985.

Letham. Lawrence. *GPS Made Easy: Using Global Positioning Systems in the Outdoors,* 3rd ed. Seattle: The Mountaineers Books, 2001.

McClung, David, and Peter Schaerer. *The Avalanche Handbook,* 2nd ed. Seattle: The Mountaineers Books, 1993.

Schad, Jerry, and David S. Moser, editors. *Wilderness Basics: The Complete Handbook for Hikers & Backpackers,* 2nd ed. Seattle: The Mountaineers Books, 1993.

Wilkerson, James A., M.D., editor, Cameron C. Bangs, and John S. Hayward. *Hypothermia, Frostbite, and Other Cold Injuries: Prevention, Recognition, Prehospital Treatment.* Seattle: The Mountaineers Books, 1986.

Wilkerson, James A., M.D., editor. *Medicine for Mountaineering & Other Wilderness Activities,* 5th ed. Seattle: The Mountaineers Books, 2001.

Index

About the Authors

Dave Felkley began his life in San Francisco in 1939. He graduated from Avalon High School on Santa Catalina Island in 1957, had a short visit at Stanford University, two years in the U.S. Army, and has been continuing his education on the trail of life ever since. After many years in the corporate automotive world, as district manager for Nissan Motor Corporation (USA) and then Mercedes-Benz of North America, he traded in his Mercedes for a pair of snowshoes, his wing tips for hiking boots, and the freeways for mountain trails. He hasn't even owned a vehicle in over 12 years, but is licensed and can rent or borrow if need be. A former mountain runner, Dave has learned to slow down to smell wildflowers and chase snowflakes under the Blue Dome, discovering material possessions are not as valuable as time. Dave is semi-retired and lives in Nederland, Colorado, at 8,500 feet in the Colorado Rockies, has three grandchildren, and prefers either to be outdoors or writing about it, as he has done through 120 columns in the local newspaper and his BIGfoot Snowshoe Tours.

Gene Prater was introduced to the art of snowshoeing at age twenty-one and used these webbed feet to enjoy winter hiking and ascend countless peaks over a period of forty-three years. He was also a sometime designer and builder of custom snowshoes and for several years led snowshoeing seminars in New England (for the Appalachian Mountain Club), the Rockies, and the Pacific Northwest. He died in 1993.

▲ *Three generations of snowshoeing Felkleys: Dave, Mack, and Doug, at an old cabin in Caribou townsite near Nederland, Colorado*